ENDORSEMENTS

My favorite verse in the Bible is Proverbs 20:7: *"The righteous man walks in his integrity; his children are blessed after him"* (NKJV). So this book excites me. Read as veteran parents/grandparents, Paul and Billie Kaye Tsika, lead us to truths that build the family with honesty and transparency.

DR. JOHNNY HUNT
Senior Pastor, First Baptist Church
Woodstock, Georgia

My wife and I have been privileged to know Paul and Billie Kaye for over thirty years. They have preached, prayed, cried, and laughed with us through our years together. We have watched our children grow through the various stages of life covered in this very important book—from a babe in our arms to married adults with children of their own.

I would encourage every young adult, married or still single, to carefully read this book, *Parenting with Purpose*, and when you have finished reading it, take the time to study and apply these great truths to your own life and marriage. You, your mate, and your children will be blessed because of your application of these truths in your everyday living.

DR. CLIFF BLACK
Pastor, Mountain Grove Baptist Church
Hickory, North Carolina

Parenting with Purpose by Paul and Billie Kaye Tsika is a powerful book of learning for both parents and children. The biblical principles are presented within the framework of practical examples for everyday living. To me, the pages of testimony of the Tsika's children best summarize the powerful example by their parents. This book is a must-read for all.

Dr. Mark A. Smith
President of Ohio Christian University
State Board of Education Member for Ohio

What an awesome resource for parents in all stages of life! This book resonates with one of the traits I have appreciated most about Paul and Billie over the years—transparency. They have driven home the point that even past failures or missed opportunities can be redeemed. One of my mentors used to say, "You can teach what you know, but you will reproduce what you are." This fantastic book literally shouts the truth of that statement. *Parenting with Purpose* outlines a strategy that, if followed, will result in improved parents and children who thrive.

Dr. Gary Hay
Pastor, Hope Church
Springfield, Missouri

Thank you, Paul and Billie Kaye and your family, for being so forthright, honest, and vulnerable in your sharing. Your candor is startling and thus so motivating! You give us, the readers, such solid instruction on how to purposefully engage with our children. A powerful reminder that God is in the restoration business, and we can ask for His help in building back that which we have neglected. As a grandfather of four, I appreciate your example to courageously engage with our grown children as they raise up their young families.

Brian F. McCoy
President and CEO
McCoy's Building Supply

Julie and I love this book! Paul and Billie Kaye dive in to the deep core of a child's heart to bring parents amazingly insightful truths and advice. We are so grateful for the lifetime of lessons, credible research, and weight of brutal honesty represented within these pages. If you want to experience all that God has destined for you in raising children, *Parenting with Purpose* is essential.

BRAD AND JULIE DUNCAN
Amway Diamond Crowns

Paul and Billie have combined the truth of the Word of God with the best insights of modern child psychology to reveal a wealth of practical application into parenting. I am convinced that this book will help you understand the love of your heavenly Father better and motivate you to express that same kind of love to your children in ways that will prepare them for their destiny!

BRIAN FIELDS
Senior Pastor, Grace Fellowship of Augusta
Augusta, Georgia

The Tsikas share many gems of wisdom about parenting "for" a purpose. These are not stand-alone anecdotes or tricks for short-term fixes. Every insightful solution is part of a plan to raise godly adults of excellence as they transition through the beginning phases of life. Paul and Billie are humble, transparent, and self-deprecating. They are willing to admit where they have gone wrong, so others can get it right.

GREG AND LAURIE DUNCAN
Amway Triple Diamonds

In an ever-changing world, as followers of Jesus Christ we are grateful to know that His Word never changes. Every day we are confronted and often called upon to compromise those biblical principles which we know have stood the test of time. Few places is this seen more frequently than in the institution of the family. More specifically, it has been most evident in the culture's parenting philosophies. This is the very reason

I am so grateful to commend to you this work of Paul and Billie Kaye Tsika. In *Parenting with Purpose*, they have invited us into their world and family. They help us discover how the principles of God's Word apply in the parenting realm and how that will yield results that will leave us inspired and encouraged. While every parent wrestles with the challenges of daily decisions, and does so knowing that we have few guarantees in life, I believe this book will help every mom and dad who seeks to win the hearts of their children.

Dr. Mark E. Harris
Senior Pastor, First Baptist Church
Charlotte, North Carolina

Strong nations are built on strong families. *Parenting with Purpose* by Paul and Billie Tsika is full of practical strategies for navigating the joyful, yet challenging process of raising children in today's world.

David Barton
WallBuilders
Author, Speaker and contributor to Fox News

PARENTING

with

PURPOSE

DESTINY IMAGE BOOKS BY PAUL AND BILLIE KAYE TSIKA

Get Married, Stay Married

PARENTING
with
PURPOSE

Winning the Heart
of Your Child

PAUL & BILLIE KAYE TSIKA

DESTINY IMAGE® PUBLISHERS, INC.
P.O. Box 310, Shippensburg, PA 17257-0310
"Promoting Inspired Lives."

This book and all other Destiny Image, Revival Press, MercyPlace, Fresh Bread, Destiny Image Fiction, and Treasure House books are available at Christian bookstores and distributors worldwide.

For a U.S. bookstore nearest you, call 1-800-722-6774.
For more information on foreign distributors, call 717-532-3040.
Reach us on the Internet: www.destinyimage.com.

ISBN 13 TP: 978-0-7684-0461-6
ISBN 13 Ebook: 978-0-7684-0462-3

For Worldwide Distribution, Printed in the U.S.A.
1 2 3 4 5 6 7 8 / 18 17 16 15 14

Don't you see that children are God's best gift?
The fruit of the womb his generous legacy?
Like a warrior's fistful of arrows
are the children of a vigorous youth.
Oh, how blessed are you parents,
with your quivers full of children!
—PSALMS 127:3-5, THE MESSAGE

DEDICATION

We would like to dedicate this book to all of those parents, grandparents, and great-grandparents who are going through that wonderful wilderness of parenting. In a day and time when parenting doesn't seem to fit the lifestyle of many, you are braving your way through by learning, growing, and changing. Congratulations on being in that unique community of responsible adults rearing the next generation. You have taken seriously God's admonishment in Psalms 127:3, *"Children a the heritage from the Lord"* (NKJV). Your labor will not be in vain, and your rewards will far outweigh your efforts.

SPECIAL DEDICATION

We want to make a very personal dedication to some very special parents and personal friends we have known through the years. Their parenting days were far too short with the passing of their beloved child.

Ron and Georgia Lee Puryear—son, Brian
Larry and Donna Swift—son, Bryan
Danny and Nancy Greig—son, Michael
Keith and Louetta Stamey—daughter, Kim
Jimmy and Sandra Hadden—daughter, Christy
Larry and Mae Mallatt—daughter, Melinda
Ron and Kaye Dunn—son, Ronald Jr.
Paul and Jerry Alaniz—son, Paul
Joe and Norma Foligo—son, Nick
Doug and Sharon Custer—son, Christopher

And there are others too numerous to mention. Your burden has been great. As we remember these friends, the words of Paul the apostle always come to mind. The apostle Paul said that we do sorrow, but not as those that have no hope. Thank God, because of Christ, we have hope in this life and the life beyond.

PAUL AND BILLIE KAYE

ACKNOWLEDGMENTS

Our first acknowledgment is to our wonderful Lord Jesus, who has given us the wisdom, strength, and grace to share our parenting story. To God be the glory, great things He has done.

To our three amazing children for all their love, patience and support in writing this book. Thank you for educating us while we were rearing you.

Mark and Gretchen Tsika Rush
Paul II and Melanie Tsika
Thom and Kelley Tsika

Destiny Image Publishers, Inc.

Our team, lead by Mykela Krieg, has made our job easy. They have been there for us with their encouragement, insight, and expertise. Thank you for another job well done. www.destinyimage.com

Rick Killian

This is the second project we have worked on with Rick. He has proven to be invaluable with his biblical insights and tireless efforts. His recommendations, patience, and labor to pull "Parenting" together in a readable form have made our labor a joy. Thank you, dear friend. www.killiancreative.com

Terry and Kaye Jackson

They have been dear friends for over 40 years. As a pastor, counselor, teacher, and not-so-good golfer, Terry has been a tremendous blessing over the course of our ministry. His wife Kaye is a very gifted singer and godly wife/mother/grandmother who has made a difference. Through the years they have developed materials that have made a significant contribution to this book. Thank you, Terry and Kaye, for always being there. www.lovequestfamilyministries.org

CONTENTS

FOREWORD

I can remember vividly the early morning that our first child was born. We had anticipated his arrival with great joy. Everything was great until they placed that little boy in my arms for the first time. I lost it! I could not identify nor control the many emotions running through me. I do remember thinking, "Oh my, this little guy will live eternally and I have been given the responsibility of stewarding his development." I uttered a prayer that went something like, "O God, I hope You know how to rear children, because I sure don't." Paul and Billie Kaye Tsika's *Parenting with Purpose* is written for such parents. They get it! Parenting is a fabulous privilege with the potential for almost unlimited joy, but it is a responsibility that if neglected has grave consequences.

We spend a lot of time fussing about the direction of the younger generation. That time should be spent parenting those who will lead that generation. Each of us is given a garden, like Adam and Eve. Included in that garden are the children who are under our care. When we tend our garden according to God's design, it grows and is healthy. If we neglect His Word and design, destruction enters and the garden becomes a wilderness. Parenting is neither optional nor inconsequential. It affects the whole world.

Sadly, we live in a day of such theological and psychological confusion that parents aren't sure what to do. Babies are too often killed or thrown away by those who see them as inconvenient. Men impregnate women and leave as if there is no responsibility on their part. But that is the tip of the iceberg. The vast majority of parents are just not sure what they are to do. It is easy to produce offspring, but not as easy to rear them to be healthy, functioning people. Babies are cute and fun to watch, but they grow up. Devoid of biblical wisdom, many parents are all over the board as they resort to various TV shows promoting the latest fad in rearing children. Without a truth filter, they get conflicting and confusing information and often end up with no definitive plan and unsure of their purpose.

I am thrilled that two responsible and honest parents have given us a no-nonsense approach to finding purpose in parenting. Paul and Billie Kaye acknowledge their own failures and mistakes, while giving confident instruction that can be understood and applied. I have known these two for thirty years. I know their children. They can be trusted. They are not writing books to make money or a name for themselves. They are writing out of a heart of love. They genuinely want to see families enjoy each other and grow together with a purpose. They believe that we can actually enjoy our children, and they have a plan that leads to that goal. They make it clear that parenting is not that complex, but you do need to know where you are going and a way to get there. They magnify simplicity, consistency, and honesty. As I read the manuscript, I thought about how much we needed this when we first became parents. I rejoice that in this generation, it is available.

DUDLEY HALL
Founder and President of
Successful Christian Living Ministries
http://www.sclm.org/

PREFACE

As Billie Kaye and I were putting the final touches on this book, we had a thought I'd like to share. Having your morning coffee with the one you love overlooking the beautiful ocean at Palm Beach, Florida can be very inspiring. On one side there is the Atlantic and on the other side a bustling city full of life. I turned to Billie and said, "Do you know the only thing that will come to a grinding halt on planet earth when we pass?"

She replied, "What?"

I said, "Us!"

All of our activities, all our travel, and all our time with our family and friends will come to an end. However, life goes on.

As true as that may be, we will leave something significant behind— our influence. The investments we have made in our children will pass on generationally. As we look at our children and see who they are becoming and observe their children, our hearts are full. They have benefitted from the mistakes that we have made and their children are better off for that.

Yes, we've made mistakes that we share in this book, but in spite of that God has blessed us with great children. We really believe more than ever before that God's grace is to look at the heart more than what seems to be apparent to us. And, if your heart is to truly win the heart of your child, then you will capture the heart of God.

Whether you're first-time parents, parents with many children, a single parent, or grandparents raising your children's children, this book is for you.

Because our children are a God-given gift, He allows us the wonderful privilege of rearing them. So have the grace to correct your mistakes, ask forgiveness, love your children the way God loves you, and "Parent with Purpose."

INTRODUCTION

Train up a child in the way he should go, and when he is old he will not depart from it. —PROVERBS 22:6 NKJV

When we hold one of our children in our arms for the first time, there is no question that they are a gift from God. However, years later, too many of us get caught in the conundrum of whether that gift was meant as a blessing or a curse! How did we get from the precious bundle of joy to the sassy, back-talking teenager? Suddenly we are wondering, "What were we thinking when we decided to have kids?" Had we only known!

Billie and I have counseled married couples for several years now, and we often find that in counseling marriages, we are counseling parents—and they have so many questions about dealing with their kids! A good friend of ours, Ron Dunn, said it best: "The challenge with raising children is, by the time you are experienced, you are unemployed."

That is exactly how we felt as we "graduated" out of parenting our three children—Gretchen, Paul Edward, and Thom. Only as they began their adult lives did we get our first glimpses of what the parenting journey had been all about. Only as we looked back over their years growing up did we see the full spectrum of what it meant to be parents, understand where we made mistakes, what we did right, and what we would have done differently had we only known. The good news is, though, our parenting didn't end there. Through a great deal of honesty with ourselves and our kids, we have built great relationships with our adult children and their families, and we have been able to help them from what we learned being their parents. It is now our pride and joy that they have built tremendous, resilient, and well-balanced families of their own.

Because of what we have learned through all of this, we can say with absolute confidence that children are gifts from God, but they are gifts who challenge us and force us to grow even as we challenge them and help them to mature. God gives us children not only to propagate humanity, but also as part of our own process of becoming all that God has planned for *us* to be. Parenting is a learning process. If we do it right, being a parent is a tremendous blessing not only for our families, but also for the world with which our families interact. There is no prouder day than when we see the children we raised become self-controlled, moral, wise, successful, and responsible adults and parents in their own rights—individuals contributing to making the world a better place.

Psalm 127 likens children to arrows in the quiver of their parents. We believe that is a fitting analogy. Parents launch their children into the future as they aim for a distant bull's-eye. Some parents take clear aim and their arrows are well directed toward their children's future mark. Other arrows are fired from unsteady bows, because parents are ambivalent about where they themselves came from and are uncertain of their aim. They tragically prove the adage, "If you aim at nothing, you will surely hit it."

Arrows must be properly cared for and protected from harm or they will not fly straight. They must be skillfully aimed or they will not hit their targets. While each arrow has properties of its own, it is also very dependent upon the marksmanship of the person releasing it. Good marksmen and markswomen are patient, disciplined, confident, and calm as they go about their craft—and the more they possess these qualities, the straighter their arrows fly. So it is with being parents.

We don't consider ourselves experts on parenting in the way most experts are determined. We don't have university degrees or doctorates in psychology or child development. We haven't written volumes of books on the subject (in fact, this is our first). Quite honestly, we made a lot of mistakes as parents raising our kids. If anything, though, we do have advanced degrees in parenting from the School of Hard Knocks. We have learned from the things that we did wrong, but even more importantly, we have experienced the power of correcting those mistakes and what that knowledge can do for others. We've learned how to heal whatever rifts we caused with our children from whatever we did that might have been hurtful. At the same time, we've also learned a great deal about the power of what we did right. Love not only covers a multitude of sins (see 1 Pet. 4:8), but also has the power to restore and strengthen relationships. Without it, no family is ever what it could be. It is why our relationships with our children and their families are stronger today than they have ever been.

While we know of no instant fixes, we have learned some time-tested principles and practices that, employed with patience, persistence, and love, can make all the difference in the world to married couples and families. As ministers and counselors for more than four decades now, we have also had the opportunity to share these with thousands, get their input, and see them influence hundreds of families for the better. What we want to share with you in these pages are not theories and ideas that sound good, but attitudes and habits we have seen work time and again with parents of varying backgrounds and belief systems.

Parenting must be approached with a plan and a perspective that allows you to get to know your children, understand their unique purposes and aspirations in life, discipline them, and prepare them for the world they will one day affect. Despite the occasional differences of opinion that are normal to life, we should enjoy loving and edifying relationships throughout that process. It's not rocket science, but it's not like falling off a log either. It takes persistence, a small toolbox of options for those wonderful times your kids stump you, and a healthy sense of both humility and purpose. (A good sense of humor doesn't hurt, either!) With these, working from early childhood through adolescence into young adulthood, you'll still have some tough lessons—children are humans in training, after all, and have a marvelous way of testing our limits as they test their own—but these practices and principles will keep you close enough to be able to talk such experiences through and come out better on the other side. They will also help your children learn the right things from those challenges, whatever they may be. They will help you see just how your children are indeed gifts meant to bless and not to curse. They will help you grow up and become a better person yourself, and teach you the fullness of joy families are supposed to experience.

We are very proud of all of our children and the decisions they are making for their lives today. As we review this manuscript for its final draft, we are in Cancun celebrating the twenty-fifth wedding anniversary of Paul Edward and Melanie. We celebrated Gretchen and Mark's twenty-fifth last year in Asheville, North Carolina. Our youngest, Thom, cautioned us to make certain we stay alive long enough to celebrate his and Kelley's twenty-fifth two years from now. We also just became great-grandparents for the first time and are looking forward to more of the same. We know that we have been greatly blessed, but we also know it's all and only because of God's grace. We have made more than our share of mistakes, and we share this book knowing the heartbreak that so many others have experienced. It is our hope that what we have learned along the way will be a source of wisdom and encouragement for those facing the tests and trials all parents face.

Every parent experiences challenges in raising children; after all, it's the first time we've ever done it. As Billie Kaye has often said, "We were children ourselves raising children." We would all make different choices if given a second chance, but we've learned from our mistakes and used that learning to try to help our children do better. We hope what we have learned can help you remember the important things about parenting and to not only instill in your children what they need to be successful in life, but to build relationships with them that will stand the tests of a lifetime.

In the end, children grow up to be adults and adults are responsible for the choices they make. We've known children who were raised in the best of homes who have turned out incorrigible and irresponsible—and children raised in the worst of homes who've turned out mature and conscientious. So don't beat yourself up. If you're wrong, say, "I'm sorry," and start again. If you're right, say, "I love you." If you're not certain if you're right or wrong, call on the Lord as we are told in Jeremiah 33:3, *"Call to Me and I will answer you, and I will tell you great and mighty things, which you do not know."* He will help you sort things out.

In our marriage book, *Get Married, Stay Married*, we said, "The heart of the problem is the problem of the heart." That's true in marriage, in life, and in raising children. We hope this book will aid you in your quest for your children's hearts. It is not about behavior modification, it's about heart changes that lead to better relationships and lives. So be encouraged as you engage in the wonderful world of *Parenting with Purpose*—if you approach it in the right way, a world of wonderful memories and priceless rewards are in store for you and your loved ones.

PAUL and BILLIE KAYE

Chapter One

BUILDING BETTER KIDS

We need to examine our parenting paradigm. Raising children has come to look more and more like a business endeavor and less and less like an endeavor of the heart. We are overly concerned with "the bottom line," with how our children "do" rather than with who our children "are." We pour time, attention, and money into insuring their performance, consistently making it to their soccer game while inconsistently making it to the dinner table. The fact that our persistent and often critical involvement is well intended, that we believe that our efforts ultimately will help our children to be happy and to successfully compete in a demanding world, does not lessen the damage.[1] —MADELINE LEVINE, PH.D.

There is no question that raising children in today's world has challenges no other generation has faced. It seems as if the Information Age has turned the generation gap into a generation canyon. With the high-speed information freeway plugged straight into our computers, cell phones, MP3 players, and now even our televisions, cultural changes are taking place faster than ever before. All these influences can make it appear nearly impossible to raise children with the right value system and to instill in them uncompromising ethics, character, and integrity. Is it still possible to ensure they have the self-control and emotional intelligence to not only succeed in life, but also make their world a better place?

Regardless of these societal pressures and rapid changes, we want you to know that there are still timeless principles that transcend any economy, any culture, any age, any political climate, and any influence from any source. As life gets faster, applying them may look a little different from in the past, but we still deal with the same issue of who we are as human beings and what we need to become in order to succeed. Whereas in the distant past, connections between parents and children were somewhat worked into the fabric of daily life on the farm or homestead, today's technological "hunter/gatherer" society demands parents be away more and travel farther to provide for their families. The stay-at-home mom is a luxury very few can afford anymore. Not only does this greatly reduce the time we have with our children, but once we are home, our kids' hectic schedules of practices, lessons, activities, and play dates often leave us little time to connect with them other than brief interactions in the car.

Because of this, the time we have as modern parents with our children is at a higher premium than ever, and how we relate to our kids during these times is even more important. We, as parents, need to know what we are about and what we are hoping to instill in our children. What commonly happens, however, is that we don't have a clear target for what kind of adults we want our children to become, and therefore don't have a blueprint for what kind of parents we should be. While we meticulously plan our careers and go the extra mile to provide for our families, what thought do we give to the more important principles and practices of building better kids and closer marriages? As the old saying goes, "If you fail to plan, you are planning to fail."

While we might have vague notions about our children one day becoming doctors or lawyers—or perhaps professional athletes, astronauts, or the President of the United States—the present generation of parents seems to have little time to consider what kinds of human beings our kids should grow up to be. More than anything else, character and a sense of divine purpose are being lost in the shuffle. Modern society is conditioning us not to even think in terms of personality qualities anymore. Instead, we micromanage for success according to the "bottom line"—grade point averages, win-loss records, class ranking, and how many activities, lessons, and sports we have our kids signed up for at one time.

So if we do work toward goals on our kids' behalf, we think of getting them into the best schools, hiring the right tutors or private coaches, connecting them with the right people, earning the biggest scholarship, and encouraging them to be at the top of every activity they are involved in—on the championship soccer team, captain of the debate team, valedictorian of their high school, voted "most likely to succeed," etc., etc. Those are all great things, but is that what is best for who our kids will one day be? Are we pinning ribbons on their chest that we have done more to earn for them than they have? Or are we developing a heart for making a difference and the personal character required for them be all God has planned for them to be?

Too many are neglecting to instill the character, skills, and qualities that will act as the means of making our children's accomplishments worthwhile. While we may desire that our child be the leader of a nation, we don't hope that he or she will be the next Hitler or Wall Street executive imprisoned for fraud! We seem to forget that our children, as the gifts of God that they are, have God-given purposes for great and wonderful things—regardless of the variety or quantity of activities we engage them in. In many ways, they are not really our children, but they are on loan to us from Heaven to accomplish whatever destiny He has already ordained for them. We are but temporary caretakers, stewards, or guardians. Each child has a destiny given by God greater than whatever we dream for our children.

As such, what do we teach our kids about being good people? About knowing God? About finding purpose in life? And what do we do to guarantee they are going to be the type of human beings God can use to do His will and bless the earth? Will they have the character quali-ties they need to find balanced success in all the arenas of life—career, family, finances, spirituality, marriage, and social/community influence? Will they have the self-control, the wisdom, the willingness to take responsibility, the respect for authority, the maturity, the relationship skills, the integrity, and the emotional, social, and moral intelligence they need not only to attain some form of success, but also to be the type of person in the midst of that success who brings honor to God and brings out the best in those around them? This may seem like a lot, but in truth, it all boils down to instilling in our children character, a sense of purpose, and a recognition of their responsibility to steward the talents they possess.

How do we accomplish that? Well, we need to look into the future and discern the distant target at which we are aiming each child. We need to get a picture of what our children should look like by the time we are getting ready to send them out of our homes into the world. What activities and traits will actually help us get them to hit that distant bull's-eye? Are we aiming them correctly or just filling up their schedules to keep them busy and "out of our hair"?

The good news is that we are not without help in answering this question or sighting into those distant targets. There has been a good deal of research on this over the years addressing these same questions, and when that is combined with the wisdom we already have from the Bible, we get a very solid picture of what we would like our children to become as they grow up under our care and authority. One of the best and most widely respected "blueprints" for godly child development we have found comes from the Search Institute. Founded in 1958 by the Lutheran Brethren, they began studying kids in church youth groups to see what attributes, activ-ities, and values contributed the most to the healthy development of children and young people. Since that time, they have opened their studies to include children and young people of all different backgrounds, ethnicities, and socioeconomic levels. Their guiding question for the last six decades has been, "What helps children and adolescents become caring, responsible, successful adults?"

From their research, they have compiled the "40 Developmental Assets®." They have found that the more of these assets children have in their lives, the more likely they are to do the things that lead to becoming successful adults. At the same time, the fewer of these assets children have, the more likely it is they will participate in rebellious, abusive, and anti-social behaviors. Though the description of each asset differs slightly depending on the developmental stage of each child, the assets do not greatly change as the child matures through adolescence. Take a look at the following checklist and see how many of these are in the life of your child:[2]

EXTERNAL ASSETS

Support

1. Children experience the support of their family.
2. There are positive communication patterns in the family.
3. There are three to five non-parent adults kids can depend upon.
4. They have caring neighbors.
5. There is a caring climate in childcare and educational settings.
6. Parents are actively involved in childcare and educating their children.

Empowerment

1. Their community cherishes and values children and youth.

2.   Children and youth are seen as contributing resources to community welfare.

3.   They take part in service to others.

4.   They feel safe in their normal settings at school, home, etc.

Boundaries and Expectations

1.   Their family has clear and established behavioral boundaries.

2.   Their childcare or schools have clear and established behavioral boundaries.

3.   There are clear and established boundaries in their neighborhood.

4.   They have positive adult role models.

5.   They have positive peer relationships.

6.   They are encouraged and expected to do their best in whatever they are doing.

Constructive Use of Time

1.   They have regular unstructured time to play and create.

2.   They spend two or fewer nights a week outside of the home.

3.   They take part in community programs outside of the home.

4.   They are part of a religious community.

INTERNAL ASSETS

Commitment to Learning

1.   They are motivated to master the skills they are being taught.

2.   They actively engage in opportunities to learn.

3. There is a connection between activities inside and outside of the home.

4. They bond well with others in their schools, clubs, and other groups.

5. They learn to read at a young age and read regularly for pleasure.

Positive Values

1. They show empathy and understanding for others.

2. They express age-appropriate concern for equality and social justice.

3. They have the courage to stand up for what they believe in.

4. They are truthful even when it is not easy.

5. They are responsible.

6. They show self-control and restraint.

Social Competencies

1. They are able to plan activities and make decisions for themselves.

2. They have sound and growing interpersonal skills.

3. They express cultural awareness and sensitivity.

4. They can resist peer pressure and recognize risky behaviors as undesirable.

5. They learn to peacefully resolve conflicts with others.

Positive Identity

1. They feel that they have an appropriate level of control over themselves and their lives.

2. They view themselves positively and feel loved.

3. They have a sense of purpose that grows as they mature.

4. They look forward to their futures.

We urge you to bookmark these pages and refer back to them often in order to get a firm picture of what each of these means for your children. Or, you can visit the Search Institute website (www.search -institute.org) to print out PDFs of these assets to discuss with your children and see which assets they feel they have and which they don't. Their website will also give you suggestions for how to develop each of these assets in your children and family environment.

Notice that the first entries on this list are all about relationships, especially each child's relationship with his or her parents. Virtually all of a child's social learning as they grow from infancy comes first through their relationships with healthy adults before it does through peers. Also, notice that while the assets support children doing their best in everything they do, nowhere is listed the need for a certain grade point average, sports ability, musical talent, or a certain number of Bible verses they should have memorized by a certain age—not that any of those are bad things, but we want you to see the focus is on character rather than achievement. Participation is emphasized over success, while at the same time "down time" used for something other than television, video games, or homework is highly valued. Being bored, as it turns out, is incredibly character building for your kids, because it forces them to be creative and use their imaginations rather than always looking outside of themselves for how to behave or what to focus upon.

Other research we have found very insightful is regarding the importance of family mealtimes. Evidence suggests that families who regularly eat dinner together (*regularly* meaning three or more times a week) have children who are less likely to be overweight, will eat healthier food, have less delinquency, are less likely to abuse alcohol or drugs, show greater academic achievement, exhibit healthier psychological well-being, and have more positive family interactions.[3] While researchers are still pondering which specific aspects of eating together are responsible for such outcomes, common sense can go a long way in figuring out that having a sit-down meal with most or all of the family members present, including everyone eating the same food and participating in conversation, is healthy for everyone. Meals provide frequent opportunities to share low-pressure, unstructured time together to interact. Conversation around the table—and even a little healthy debate from time to time—does wonders for developing relationship skills and individual convictions. In short, eating meals together offers a great atmosphere for you to rub off on your kids bit by bit.

Some of the most wonderful times we have enjoyed with our children have been around the dinner table. Even though we have had a few negative experiences through the years (none of them because of Billie's cooking), the vast majority of our meals together have been times of great fellowship. When our kids were growing, we used to have regular "camp meetings" in our area—times when preachers, singers, and missionaries would come together and celebrate the Lord—and we would have out-of-town guests over to our home for meals. We have also had private concerts in our home by some of the most well-known Christian singers and groups, as well as hosted prominent pastors, evangelists, and missionaries. We often had more than fifty at a time, and our children loved listening to their stories and asking them questions. The children felt acknowledged, blessed, and honored to be part of that company. They still talk about those wonderful times today.

We have carried that tradition on at Restoration Ranch where we live now. Whenever we have company, the whole family gathers to enjoy very special times around the meal table. Even when there's no company, our children and grandchildren gather frequently at the Lodge to eat together. Mimi's (Billie's) kitchen is always open to our family, even though the sign she has posted may not reflect that. It simply reads:

CHILDREN BY APPOINTMENT ONLY;

GRANDCHILDREN WELCOME ANYTIME.

We love to sit and listen to the interaction between our children and grandchildren around the big table in our dining room. We can learn so much, because it's a safe environment for them to be themselves, express their ideas, and learn from the perspectives and experiences of each other. We have laughed, cried, expressed concerns, helped guide their thinking, and had our thinking guided by them—all around a table set by love with fellowship as the main course.

THE BOTTOM LINE

The long and short of it is that better kids—and therefore, better human beings—are built with the same ingredients they always have been:

- loving parents who set reasonable limits,
- enforce those limits,
- guide their kids into activities and interactions where they can learn and experiment on their own in healthy ways,
- allow them to solve their own problems,
- encourage them to do their best,
- talk with them on a regular basis, and
- love them no matter what.

If there have been any changes over the decades since we were kids, it is not in the basics of being a parent as much as it is that parents are squeezed by all kinds of new influences and time constraints. These can cause parents to have fewer interactions with their children, be tempted to lower standards to reduce conflict, to placate rather than discipline, to feel inadequate about themselves as parents and overcompensate by doing too much for their kids, and any number of other things that are getting in the way of helping kids mature and flourish. We believe that the foundation upon which we build healthy families is fivefold:

1. Spiritually—how we each relate to God.

2. Relationally—how we relate to each other.

3. Emotionally—how each of us relates to ourselves.

4. Physically—how we relate to the body God gave us.

5. Historically—how we relate to our heritage.

Every child needs a solid family heritage as a foundation upon which to build their self-image and against which to contrast their decisions. Common sense as well as research tells us that a vital element for building a family is instilling a healthy sense of personal history—an appreciation for one's roots and the values that make up who we are, both naturally and spiritually. Most children today have no sense of continuity or regard for family history. They feel like they don't know where they come from, and they don't know where they are going.

As parents, having a picture in our mind of where we hope our children will one day be—working with God to discover and release their unique gifts and calling—will go a long way to giving them a solid heritage, so they will know not only where they are going, but why. There is really no greater gift we can give our children—or the world they will someday change for the better.

NOTES

1. Madeline Levine, *The Price of Privilege: How Parental Pressure and Material Advantage Are Creating a Generation of Disconnected and Unhappy Kids* (New York: HarperCollins Publishers, 2006), 14.

2. For more information, age-specific descriptions, and suggested activities to develop each individual asset in your child, see the Search Institute's website at http://www.search-institute.org (accessed May 24, 2013). The 40 Developmental Asset® are used with permission from Search Institute, Minneapolis, MN.

3. Eliza Cook and Rachel Dunifon, "Do Family Meals Really Make a Difference?" Cornell University, College of Human Ecology, http://www.human.cornell.edu/pam/outreach/parenting/research/upload/Family-Mealtimes-2.pdf (accessed May 27, 2013).

Chapter Two

A FIRM FOUNDATION

A saint's life is in the hands of God like a bow and arrow in the hands of an archer. God is aiming at something the saint cannot see, and He stretches and strains, and every now and again the saint says—"I cannot stand any more." God does not heed, He goes on stretching till His purpose is in sight, then He lets fly.[1] —OSWALD CHAMBERS

One of the most important things we have learned about parenting over the years is that it is a process of growth and course correction, both for our children and us as parents. Children, in fact, only become better human beings as their parents become better human beings—and, for that matter, better parents. Being a parent increases our capacity to love, be patient, become more organized, discipline our own habits, control our tempers, and so much more because parenting pushes us to our limits and tests our resolve in so many ways.

How successful we are as parents has a great deal to do with how we respond to the challenges of parenting. The sturdiness of a ship is not tested in smooth waters, but in rough seas. The same can be said of a family. In order for us to respond correctly when the first wave crashes over the bow, we need a good plan and a positive outlook to carry us through. Again, we need to begin with the end in mind—with a sense of direction and desired destination. If we are going to hit the target of our children becoming resilient, responsible, and contributing adults, we have to know where we are aiming them!

For most people, the default style of parenting is that we raise our children as an afterthought, absorbed with our own aspirations, priorities, and desires. This mode of operation causes us to do things pretty much the same way our parents raised us, whether those practices were good or bad—or we default into the other autopilot mode, which is to do the exact opposite of what our parents did, because we don't like the way we were raised. The problem with both of these approaches is that they happen without the formation of a reasonable strategy based on what we value and believe. Even if our parents did do things incorrectly, just doing the opposite isn't going to make life with our own children any better. If we want a better childhood for our kids, we have to have a real plan and a proper perspective from which to apply it. We must understand the nature of our children, who they were created to be, and how to balance their needs and personal growth with our own. We have to find a way to recognize where we are heading as well as enjoy the journey on the way together.

While most parents plan to have children, very few plan their children's journeys into adulthood. It's as if holding our babies in our arms is the end of a process rather than the beginning of one. A parent certainly goes through a lot (especially Mom!) to see a baby born healthy, but the next eighteen years are pretty important too! Our infants are going to change dramatically and quickly in the next few months and years—are we ready for those changes? Do we have a goal in mind for how we are going to navigate those changes? Do we even have an idea of what they're going to be? Do we have a map of where we want them to go as far as behavior, temperament, and demeanor? Do we know the milestones along the way?

If we look around, there is a lot of good information and advice for how to develop such a map and for navigating its tough spots successfully. God has not left us without instruction or examples on how to instruct our children and nurture our families. After all, it's not as if you are the first to have ever parented—it is just your first trip through it. Countless generations have done it before and learned some valuable lessons to pass along in the process. We know that listening to previous generations can work wonders because it has for our own adult children and their families. We know it can for you and yours as well.

That is one of the reasons we like the quote by Oswald Chambers at the beginning of this chapter, as it echoes the metaphor of Psalm 127 and what we believe parenting is all about. God knows what He is doing in developing us to fulfill our purposes in life, and He knows what He is doing in developing our children to do what He is calling them to do. In fact, part of that plan is that we would be their parents. He knew what He was doing when He gave us our children. He has a plan. All we have to do is tap into it and follow His instructions.

And God knows how to be a parent—we don't call Him "our Father" for nothing! In fact, we know of no better example of being a parent than God the Father. He nurtures and counsels each of us toward becoming all He created us to be. He is at times the loving disciplinarian: *"For those whom the Lord loves He disciplines"* (Heb. 12:6); at other times He encourages us to come to Him calling out *"Abba* [or we would say, "Daddy"], *Father"* (Rom. 8:15). He is the One who has made *"plans for* [our] *welfare and not for calamity to give* [us] *a future and a hope"* (Jer. 29:11), and who said to Jeremiah, *"Before I shaped you in the womb, I knew all about you. Before you saw the light of day, I had holy plans for you"* (Jer. 1:5 MSG). The Bible even tells us children are *"fearfully and wonderfully made"* (Ps. 139:14).

God knows there is a huge difference between children and adults (by the way, the "growing up" process has been part of His plan from the beginning), and that while we are young it is best that we are set under teachers and guardians, within rules and structures, that we might understand the basics of right and wrong. From there we must grow up into grace in order to live in real freedom and move toward fulfilling our potential. He wants to help us learn to make good decisions, unencumbered by the entanglements of bad habits or wrong desires that drag us down and keep us from succeeding and living the abundant life He desires for us.

We once heard our friend, author, and conference speaker Jack Taylor say it this way, "God didn't give you your children for what you can do for them. He gave you your children for what they can do for you." We believe that we are all clay in the Potter's hands, and children are malleable "lumps" the Master molds and shapes into vessels of honor with the help of the parents, if we are sensitive to His leadings. In the process, as we work with God, we are also molded into more of what He has always hoped we would be.

THE GIFT OF A CHILD

This is how we know that children are gifts from God specifically picked out for each of us. They are blessings, but that doesn't mean they come "perfect" and don't demand careful nurturing, structured discipline, or active training to become all they are supposed to be. Then as we provide those parameters for our children, the process helps us to grow and mature as well.

You could say there are two perspectives of what children are when they come to us. Some people see them as seeds we plant in the garden that need to be watered, cared for, and nurtured until they bear fruit. Other people see them like new cars. They are perfect the day they roll off the showroom floor, and we have to do everything we can to protect their pristine "newness" and innocence. The truth of the matter is, they are a little of both. On one side, there is an innocence that needs to be protected from bad influences around them in the world. We have to "condition" them to resist damage from the storms of life or ingesting the wrong things. On the other side, however, they have a tremendous potential bred into them that will only come out if we allow them to grow and change. There is a destiny they need to be nurtured into realizing. Without careful intervention, that potential will wither and die. We must pay attention to both of these aspects if we are to raise them to be all they can be.

One of the biggest stumbling blocks of modern society is that our pace of life often leaves parents feeling at least a little negligent, and thus a little guilty that we haven't spent more time with our children. There are many things we may do to overcome that guilt. For example, when we make the time to be with them, especially when they are young, the last thing we want to do is spend that time correcting or disciplining them. Add to that the ease with which young children are appeased, manipulated, intimidated, or bribed into submission, and you will see the beginning of the trend we have today. Children aren't disciplined when they are younger, because placating them is easier in the short term than more structured discipline. The trouble is, that is a recipe for disaster when your kids grow to the point you can no longer tuck them under your arms and take them to their rooms.

If we have difficulties with our older children—and we mean big difficulties, not just the day-to-day childish stuff that comes with them making mistakes or getting a little too uppity from time to time—we believe it is because we did not put in the time and apply the appropriate structure and guidance when our children were younger. Those parents who have a plan and a structure for their children when they are younger get to experience the truth that if you

> *Train up a child* [note that says "child," not "teen"] *in the way he should go, and when he is old* [or enters adolescence and then adulthood] *he will not depart from it* (Proverbs 22:6 NKJV).

When asked about how he created his magnificent statue of David from a quarried mass of marble, Michelangelo historically said, "In every block of marble I see a statue as plain as though it stood before me, shaped and perfect in attitude and action. I have only to hew away the rough walls that imprison the lovely apparition to reveal it to the other eyes as mine see it." This is a great metaphor for parenting as well as sculpting. As we get insight into who our children are as God sees them, it is our job to skillfully "hew away" the parts that will confine or encumber who they are to become. That allows the "masterpiece" God put into them to be revealed to the world. (And, of course, it sounds so easy when you say it like that, though it will take us more than the eighteen years we have them in our homes to bring out all they are supposed to be!)

FEARFULLY AND WONDERFULLY MADE

Children are, in many ways, born as raw, unshaped "blocks," at least emotionally, intellectually, and spiritually. While they have some miraculous qualities from the beginning and genetic traits integrated into their every cell, science is learning more and more that those inborn characteristics are not as deterministic as some would suggest. Neither nature nor nurture have exclusive rights to creating who a child will become, but rather they work together and often complement each other, if parents are sensitive to them. Within the "marble" are innate characteristics that must be understood for the masterpiece to emerge. At the same time, if left to themselves, they never become more than they were at the beginning—immature, selfish, and naïve. God put a work of art into each of them; however, it is the craftsman's job to "nurture" it out (hopefully according to the original Designer's plan).

One such trait that we must address is that, no matter how cute and cuddly our children are at birth, they are always born into the world completely self-absorbed—a trait that will serve them well in infancy, but must be gradually tempered with the virtues of love, self-control, and moral judgment. While infants are absolutely consumed with their own desires to be fed, cleaned, dried, and comforted, they also have an innate need to connect with those around them—otherwise, how will they ever get those needs met? Thus, God created them to be "cute" to draw our attention. They are programmed to cry when they have a need. Then, when we respond, within that relationship to their parents and caregivers children begin to learn. The brain begins to understand how to interpret the input of the five senses from the distance of a parent's face to the baby's as it lies in the crook of our elbow—the natural distance between a mother and an infant suckling at her breast.

In these earliest months, babies learn in a process Harvard researchers call "serve and return." Babies cry, coo, wiggle, make facial expressions, babble, and gesture expressing themselves and calling out for what they need from the world. Then the caregivers respond and "correct," often meeting children halfway in the very natural action of reaching out to them and approximating their expressions back to them, but in a slightly more socially understood manner. If the child cries, the parent responds by seeing if he or she is hungry or needs to be changed. The child reaches out, and the adult places a finger in the tiny hands for the infant to grasp. The child scrunches up its nose, and the adult smiles. Thus "baby talk" is not as silly as it often sounds. We are actually imitating the child's babbling and gurgling and "return" to them something more like actual speech, helping them learn language.

All the while, with every response of the caregiver, the infant brain is firing and forming neural pathways of understanding and learned behaviors. The more a child gets this stimulus and response, the more the brain develops—and the more a child is neglected and left without care and interaction, the less these pathways form. Researchers have found that the brain changes an amazing amount in the first year. By the child's first birthday, a one-year-old brain has more in common with an adult brain than with the brain the child was born with. In other words, a one-year-old brain is more like that of a twenty-year-old than that of a one-day-old.

Until infants become toddlers and can move around on their own, there is very little "discipline" needed other than this loving correction of imitating back to babies a better response and letting them know they are cared for, loved, and safe to learn and explore the world as best they can. At the same time, two-month-olds should already be able to calm themselves briefly, the first expression of self-control. Still, there's not much getting around picking up children who are crying in the middle of the night, of comforting them through sickness or teething, or responding whenever they "call." This doesn't mean babies have to be picked up the instant they cry (especially if you are angry with the baby for crying—then it is best to let the baby cry and calm yourself first), but it does mean we will go to them, see if they can calm themselves, or if there is something else we need to do for them. As a rule, you are going to be more at their beck and call than they are at yours. Thankfully, that period of their lives only lasts a matter of months.

What too often happens to the guilty or uncertain parent, however, is infants train them through this process rather than the other way around. Young parents get used to responding to their child's every whim, trying to appease or placate whatever is wrong, and as the baby grows into the walking stage, they still respond as if the child were a helpless newborn. To them, the child hasn't really changed that much—it hasn't been that long, after all—but cognitively the child has made incredible strides in understanding the world in which he or she lives and can understand much more than we give the toddler credit for. From potty training to respecting authority, it is time to start getting the child ready for the world in which he or she will live.

While there is really no call for spanking a child at this age (we will talk about spanking later, but for now suffice it to say that you can't spank a child who can't understand what is happening), we certainly believe that it is more appropriate to house-proof your children than to childproof your house. While taking certain precautions to protect your children and property in areas you would like to let your children crawl around and explore is fine, at the same time you can teach children to understand that there are things they should avoid.

One of the best ways to train your children at this age is what many call the "uh-oh" song. When you are watching them and they start off toward a place that you don't want them to be in, you simply say, "Uh oh!" Then you pick them up and put them on your knee facing away from where you don't want them to go. You then love on them a bit and put them back on the floor. If they wander in the same direction again or another undesirable direction, repeat "Uh oh" and go through the same training process again. It won't take your child long to learn that "Uh oh" means change directions. Pretty soon you just need to say "Uh oh," and your child will adjust his or her course without further help. It is also better than filling your child's world with constant, negative "*No!*" all of the time. Training in this way will take some patience and persistence, but ultimately it will give benefits for years to come.

It is also important to remember that while we may get help from outside sources—daycare workers, nannies, babysitters, relatives, etc.—the primary responsibility for guiding this process is the parents. If we don't do it, nothing any of these other people do will matter. It may get our children to behave for them, but that won't be anything that necessarily carries over to other caregivers or learning environments. While that will vary widely from child to child, the only constant for any child is his or her parent(s), and if we as parents will accept our role as primary influencers ordained by God, the child will be all the better for it.

FROM CHILDHOOD TO ADOLESCENCE

Children think very concretely throughout their first decade of life. Their thought processes tend to be more black and white, yes and no, or on and off like a light switch. Something is or it isn't. The nuances in between are just not there. For example, a friend once told us the funny story of debating with their child over the sex of the dachshund they gave him for Christmas. The boy insisted that the dog was a boy even though they assured him it was a girl. The boy responded, "But it is *my* puppy, so I get to decide whether it is a boy or a girl!" He seemed to have a fledgling understanding of property rights and ownership—and was very logical by his own standards—but did not yet have a very firm grasp of biology. As he grew, naturally, so did his understanding.

For their own protection and sense of security, children need clear rules and boundaries within which they can safely explore and experiment. As they grow older, these will broaden as they are exposed to more and more of the world around them—they go from the home to play dates with friends to preschool and then on to elementary, middle, and high school, or some progression like that. In that growth, children need to learn how to interact with others and obey those looking after or instructing them. It also means the beginning of disciplining your child in a way that can be understood by the child. Limits without consequences for violating them have no meaning. (We will deal with discipline for violating boundaries in upcoming chapters—for now we want to get an overview of how children develop cognitively as they grow and what that means for us as we parent them.)

Children develop cognitively, emotionally, socially, and intellectually at a pretty steady pace from the time they start walking until the time they approach puberty. That transition provides key milestones along the way in the discipline, upbringing, and nurturing of your child. But then all of a sudden, things speed up. As the hormones kick in that begin puberty, pre-teens face the beginning of the biggest brain change of their lives. From the beginning of puberty through the time they are about twenty-five or twenty-six (a few years less for young women), the brain makes the leap from childhood black-and-white thinking into the ability to handle the lightning-fast, complex, and multifaceted thinking of an adult. The brain starts a paring and superhighway-building phase where it eliminates unused neural pathways and enhances those that get the most traffic. This allows a tremendous acceleration of the speed of thought. These pathways become so fast that thinking along them becomes effectively instantaneous and somewhat subconscious. This enables the prefrontal cortex to take on more complicated and principled decision-making challenges and abstract thoughts. It is a little bit like memorizing the multiplication and division tables as a child so that when you tackle calculus, you don't have to stop and count out each answer on your fingers anymore before going on. The brain has faster access to all the teen has learned once the superhighway to that part of the brain is complete—the trouble is that while the highway is "under construction," sometimes you wonder if the adolescent remembers any of the common sense you taught him or her as a child.

The great problem this poses for families is that as the child is getting too big to overpower by picking them up and sitting them down in a corner, their hormones are pumping them full of new desires and emotions, all while their brain is trying to decide which patterns of thought from childhood it wants to take into adulthood. We often talk about "senior moments" where we are forgetful or feel as if our logical thinking process isn't working as it should, but we need to realize our teens are more prone to "adolescent moments" of questioning, challenging, and experimenting than we will ever experience when we are older. It is a wonderful time as our children begin to analyze all they learned as children and turn the two-dimensional concepts of childhood into the multifaceted principles that will guide their lives—it is also a horrifying time as our children begin to confront all they learned as children and begin deciding what they will believe and how they will behave for themselves. It will be a time for some of the greatest talks you will have with your kids as well as for the biggest arguments! It will also be a time when they make some incredible "judgment errors" because their brains are just not working at a peak level because they are in the midst of being rewired.

More than ever, you will need a plan to be ready for those challenges so that you can handle your teens' curveballs with an even temper, logical arguments they can understand, and a steady resolve to hang on to what you have determined in your own life is Truth. Don't be surprised if you have a "healthy" debate about a subject one day you are sure you lost, and then just a few days later hear your teen present the same line of thinking you presented as they argue with a friend over the same issue. That is the beauty of adolescents—they are good at "changing their minds" in a very literal sense!

THE BOTTOM LINE

While this is a very nutshell overview of the cognitive and developmental changes your child will see from the time they are born to their going out into the world on their own, we feel it is important to understand the basics of what is happening with your children. This way you can be ready for those personality "blips" that become learning opportunities between parent and child. When they misbehave, challenge your authority, break something, fight with a sibling, violate the rules at school, or come to you with one of those questions of the universe, such as "Where do babies come from?"—how are you as a parent going to respond? Do you have a principled plan for how you will react? When they push your buttons, are you going to lose your composure and do something you will later regret?

Believe it or not, it is not about what your kids do as much as it is about how you as a parent respond to their actions. Even in their most challenging moments, you are still a model for how they should behave. You can't really control whatever creative outburst of "personality" kids are going to come up with in a given moment, but you can decide what you are going to do in response. Will you be stunned into inaction by their tantrum in the middle of the toy aisle? Will you be so embarrassed and ashamed that you lash out at them physically? Or, will you use the opportunity to teach that tantrums are simply not expressions that will be either a) effective or b) something they want to repeat?

We, the parents, have the power to lay the foundational heritage of our families and to determine the atmosphere in our homes. While we can't control our ancestries and what we learned as our parents raised us, we can give our children a better childhood than we experienced to build their families on in the future. That will not happen unless we think through and determine some things beforehand. Thankfully, that is exactly what we are talking about in this book. By the time you finish reading, we hope you will be well on your way to having that foundation laid and be ready for those moments that make parenting so poignant—one way or the other!

The purpose of a strong foundational heritage of love, boundaries, and discipline is to give children a bedrock upon which to build lives of character, integrity, maturity, and self-direction. The world around us can throw a million different things at us, but if we understand the importance of the simple principles upon which character is built—love, joy, peace, patience, kindness, goodness, faithfulness, gentleness, and self-control (see Gal. 5:22-23)—our homes will stand through the storms of life. You will have a readiness plan for when the tornadoes of childhood hit—and because of the way you handle them with ease, you will have children you can be proud of.

NOTE

1.   Oswald Chambers, *My Utmost for His Highest: Selections for the Year* (Grand Rapids, MI: Oswald Chambers Publications; Marshall Pickering, 1986), May 8.

Chapter Three

BE THE RIGHT EXAMPLE

*There are little eyes upon you, and they're
watching night and day;
There are little ears that quickly take in every word you say;
There are little hands all eager to do all the things you do,
And a little boy who's dreaming of the day he'll be like you.*

*You're the little fellow's idol, you're the wisest of the wise;
In his little mind about you no suspicions ever rise;
He believes in you devoutly, and holds that all you do
He will say and do in your way when
he's grown up just like you.*

*There's a wide-eyed little fellow who believes
you're always right,
And his ears are always open and he watches day and night,
You are setting an example every day in all you do,
For the little boy who's waiting to grow up to be like you.*
—Author Unknown, from the 1986 *Farmer's Almanac*

I f there is one thing we have noticed in the area of parenting over the years it is this: broken parents have a tendency to make broken kids. Thank God the opposite is true as well—psychologically healthier parents tend to have psychologically healthier kids.

If you have read our book *Get Married, Stay Married*, you will know that I (Paul) had a lot of anger issues when Billie and I were first married. This not only caused communication issues with Billie, but it also bled over into my relationship with each of our children as they were growing up. Because of my personal issues, even though I loved my children, I defaulted toward punishment in their earlier years rather than sitting to talk with them about their behavior and teaching them right and wrong. This was compounded further by the fact that I was on the road so much as a traveling evangelist who spoke all across the country that I didn't have a lot of time to be with them. It seemed like when I was home I was always giving them instructions and telling them what to do. I wish I had taken more time to just listen to them and hear their hearts.

Because I had never thought it through and decided what kind of parent I wanted to be, I reacted more than I disciplined with a real aim in mind. As I got older, though, I also got wiser. God delivered me from my extreme anger, and I began a process of healing the relationships in my life. By that time, however, our children were already grown— Gretchen was out of the house and off to college, and Paul Edward was very close to that. For the most part, their childhoods were over. However, "*nothing is impossible with God*" (Luke 1:37 NLT). So, through a good deal of talk, asking for forgiveness, and patience, I was able to heal my relationships with my children. Today we love being with each other and vacation together every other year. (For more on that process, see Chapter Fourteen: Rebuilding Broken Relationships.) Needless to say, we have also spent some time healing the anger issues I passed on to my children, thankfully before they had children of their own.

The Bible calls this pattern, "*visiting the iniquity of fathers on the children and on the grandchildren to the third and fourth generations*" (Exod. 34:7). In other words, children pick up the shortcomings and weaknesses of their parents, as I did with mine and my children did with me, but God helped us bring that to a halt. As I said, broken parents have a tendency to raise broken kids, but that is a process that can be turned around through sincere dialogue, apology, and forgiveness.

When we choose to grow healthier ourselves as parents, we pave the way for healthier children. When I was able to deal with my issues, I became a better father, and that insight helped me become a better role model for my offspring as they began parenting. What I learned through my own emotional healing process allowed me to understand my anger and discuss it with my kids, thus ending an unhealthy cycle. Together we created a new cycle that has led to stronger relationships and emotionally healthier human beings throughout three different generations.

CHANGING FOR OUR CHILDREN

Many couples come to us wanting to know what they can do about their nearly adult children who are doing this or that, and our answer is frankly, "Nothing." You can't make your kids change by the time they are in their late teens or early twenties any more than you can make your spouse change. However, the good news is that there is still hope for your relationship. While you can't make *them* change, *you* can change yourself and how you behave. When we change as individuals, others often change in response. Becoming healthier human beings ourselves creates a new cycle that leads to healthier relationships. That then helps everyone in those relationships to become healthier, better human beings. So, while we can't make our older children change, we can be better examples for them—and that generally leads to better things for everyone.

When we take care of ourselves first and work to handle life in a healthier way, we change how we model handling the stresses of life for our children, and that in turn gives them better examples for how to handle whatever they face in their own lives. If we demonstrate the right kind of life, our kids will have a good chance of catching it. The negative side is that they also catch our negatives. Kids see everything; they don't miss a thing. Our children will notice our seemingly harmless indiscretions, but they will also pick up on our composure in the midst of stress and our grace for overcoming those stresses. Our strongest lessons will always be *caught* rather than *taught*, and the more we actually possess the character traits we want to instill into our children, the more easily those traits will be for them to embrace. Nothing undermines virtue more than hypocrisy—and nothing supports it better than good role models.

What we do always sends a stronger signal than what we say. Training and discipline should prepare our children to think for themselves—it should give them pause to reconsider and time to both take responsibility for their actions and rethink how they will behave in the future. When they take those pauses though, it is natural for them to look at the world around them for examples of a better way of doing things. Who do they see handling things better than they did? Who can they emulate for a better life?

Even in the midst of disciplining our kids we give them examples of how to handle the difficulties of life. How you discipline is a strong example for how you problem-solve. Do you do it coolly and calmly, or angrily and erratically? Punishment doesn't accomplish that; punishment can only make them stop and reconsider. How they think after that comes out of their relationship and dialogue with you. That, as we have already said a few times, is what discipline is all about.

Training and discipline should flow out of the atmosphere of the home. We are training our children one way or the other by the way we live before them every day. We are influencing our children one way or the other by the way we, their parents, live.

TEACH YOUR CHILDREN WELL

The person your child becomes is ultimately the product of two things:

1. His or her life experiences, including what they see others do.

2. How they interact with those experiences.

We teach our children daily by the way we own our life experiences and how we interact with them. The value system we exhibit is the one that has the greatest potential for infecting the way our children will live once they grow up. Chances are, if we continually exhibit healthy coping skills, we will empower our children to do the same—if we do not, chances are they will struggle with the issues they face unless someone else steps in to show them a better way. That, unfortunately, is the exception rather than the rule, but it did happen for us. Thank God He stepped into our lives and showed us a better way.

That is why we like to say that, "Parenting is for parents." Being a parent is first a growth process for us as adults, then for the children we have been entrusted with. God will teach you more through your children than you would learn any other way, if you will only pay attention and be open to personal growth as you help them grow and mature.

Both of us wish we had looked back at how our parents raised each of us earlier in our lives and confronted and forgiven the injustices and hurts we experienced. We should have also recognized the good things our parents did and learned to celebrate the traditions and family times that brought us all closer together. Dealing with such issues has a way of cutting off the negative cycles and encouraging the good. It clears away our default reactions to the way we were raised so that we can consciously decide how we want to raise our own children.

Another thing we wish is that we had been more transparent with our children from a much younger age. As parents, we believed that we shouldn't let our kids ever see that we had faults, that we struggled, or that we could be hurt emotionally. While there are some areas where our children really shouldn't see us sweat—like our kids should never think it is a challenge for us to handle them and their behavior—at the same time, they could have learned a great deal by going through things with us rather than always being shielded from them. We shouldn't be afraid to use examples from our own pasts—even hurts and betrayals—as illustrations of how to overcome bad things that happen to them. We should definitely use examples of where we prevailed over bitterness, anger, or shame, or learned an important lesson. Anywhere we gained a life-changing insight can be an example that will save our children grief and anxiety. Sharing examples from our own lives always carries a great deal of weight with our children. We need to be comfortable with communicating how we worked through such issues so that our children can know how to work through similar circumstances for themselves.

At the same time, remember how much traditions, family meals together, vacations, and other events you shared brought you closer and gave you stories that you still tell today. Relive stories of your grandparents with your kids that illustrate the best things about them and memories you have always cherished. This gives your children a positive heritage as well as a wealth of examples to draw from for every decision they make in their own lives.

Understand your vital role as Mom and Dad. Your example as a loving married couple before your children sets an incredibly important standard for your children's future. More of our kids today need godly examples of husbands and wives who live submitted to one another in the fear of God. While God did establish a hierarchy in the leadership of the family, He did not establish a dictatorship. Men, rather than emphasizing that the husband is in charge, you should first be an example of how to love Mom, and then each of the kids for who they are. Confident leaders guide and walk the talk; insecure leaders order and demand. Mom should then be an example of how to respect her husband, even when she doesn't always agree with what he has to say. They should work things out together, without belittling or manipulation. How you resolve differences of opinion is a powerful example to your children for how they resolve conflicts in their own lives. As married couples, we are instructed in Ephesians 5 to submit to one another, because we are in partnership to do the will of the Lord, not just in life, but also in raising and training our families. The most important relationship in the home is first that of Dad and Mom to God, then to each other, and only then to the kids. Mom and Dad should always be united, even if it seems more of a challenge today than it ever was before.

Times have certainly changed since we were young. For one thing, stay-at-home moms were the norm when we grew up. Dad went off to work each day to provide for the family. This cultural change has had a lot of different ramifications, but perhaps none has been as severe as the deterioration of the image of the American father. While this can't be blamed on women going into the workplace—and there are still many good fathers in two-income families—for sundry reasons, men are not standing up to be the fathers that our society so greatly needs.

Men need to step up to the plate, take care of their children, be there for the mothers and for their children, while also still being the pacesetters God called them to be. While societal norms continue to change, the roles of father and mother really do not. The father is still the spiritual leader in the home and the family protector. It is the father who gives the family its sense of security and identity, shows his family the importance of devotion to God, and is responsible to teach his family the Truth. A father must be a model for trust. Trust comes through relationship—a father must be a man of his word. Fathers, if you tell your children you are going to do something, back it up with your life. You should give your children the freedom to fail and learn from their mistakes, because you trust them—a father's firm trust in his children makes them want to be worthy of that trust.

Fathers are also responsible for creating the right atmosphere for godly affection. They should be good listeners. Fathers should make every effort to express their love in ways their children will understand. Dads, be affectionate, encouraging, and spend meaningful time with your families. It is the father who gives the children a proper perspective of sexuality. He should be available to answer questions, he should be accurate and specific, and he should talk to his sons about sexuality within the context of marriage. He needs to stress responsibility and respect. He can affirm his sons, especially as they enter adolescence and adulthood, and help them understand what it means to be men of honor. He can screen his daughters' dates and discuss the parameters of dating activities. He can show what is proper affection through hugs and snuggling when his children are young. Girls who know that their fathers love them and aren't afraid to hug them appropriately have fewer hang-ups or temptations when they start to date and eventually marry.

While mothers tend to be the communication hub of the family, it is still the father who makes sure communication flows correctly and freely. Fathers can call everyone together for family meetings and make sure each gets a say. He can check to see if all lines of communication are open and help the family deal with hurts and misunderstandings. These are the responsibilities of the father in the home, not the mother. A lot of moms fill that void today because dads have abdicated that role, but that is not as it should be.

Too often today men are passive and fail to embrace their roles. Despite the best efforts of the mother, things just don't work as smoothly if fathers are not actively engaged with their families. Strong wives should be a plus, not a reason to cop out. Men need to be active leaders in the home. Mothers are more likely to be engaged no matter what—even if they have busy jobs—but passive dads tend to check out and create an imbalance in the family that hurts everyone. Men need to remember who God has called them to be.

What is the mother's role? Mothers are the primary nurturers. It is generally the mom who teaches the children to give, share, and forgive. She sets the mood of all the relationships. I (Billie) remember when our children were very young, I got up in the morning and would put on praise music as the kids were getting up and preparing for school. It would set an atmosphere in the whole house. When I did that there was less friction and more peace.

Mothers also model proper intimacy. She works together with her husband as a team. She teaches sensitivity to others. She responds with special tenderness toward her children. She teaches them that it is all right to express emotions and the proper way to express them. A mother is a comforter and is particularly sensitive to the child's heart that is broken or hurt.

A mother is a safe person with whom to talk. She allows her children to be honest and vulnerable and listens without condemnation. A mother teaches her children the value of godly submission. She sees herself as her husband's helper and partner. She demonstrates respect for the father, and thus gives the father a sense of security and strength in the home.

A mother is a role model for her daughters in relating to others. At first the mother is a counselor and a guide; but later, as daughters near adulthood, Mom can become a friend. The way Mom treats Dad is a model for how her daughters will one day treat their husbands.

When our children were growing up, Paul was away a lot, so I was the one at home who was the primary disciplinarian and peace-keeper for the family. When Paul came home, I'd gladly turn it over to him. Unlike most would think, we didn't feel this adversely affected or warped our children, because we treated his need to travel as normal. I know a lot of mothers hold somewhat of a grudge against husbands who are gone a lot for work. They let that frustration and anger seep through into their attitudes by the way they speak about their husbands, even with their children, but we know from our own lives that it doesn't have to be that way.

Mothers, your attitude guides your children in so many little ways—when you are hurt or angry about something, don't think it won't affect your kids, because you are the heart of the home. The way you respond to difficult situations makes all the difference in the world. You have the choice to get bitter about your husband being gone frequently, or you can explain to your children, "Listen, Daddy is building us a life. He is doing this because he loves us. He is building something for our future."

The way you respond and honor your husband will teach your children how to respond to adversities in their own lives.

I (Paul) was gone about eight out of the first eleven years of our family's life—that means I missed birthdays, first words, first steps, so many things—but you know what? It didn't warp our children because of Billie's attitude. She saw me being gone as paying a price and sacrificing to build something for our future. While I don't endorse being gone so much if you don't have to be—I do regret missing so much of our kids' growing up— but I am saying that is the route we had to go and our children are doing great today because of Billie's attitude. Never once did I hear a complaint from her about me having to travel so much. Never once did she tell me I ought to be at home more. Never once did she grumble to me on the phone so that I felt guilty and couldn't focus on what I was called to do.

That is why we encourage a mother to remain positive in situations where her husband has to be gone a great deal. Maybe you are a military family. Maybe your husband has a traveling sales job. Maybe he is a traveling minister like Paul was. When your husband is out there doing what he is doing to build a life and a future, if you will speak well of him and encourage your children about what he is doing, you set an example for them that they will never forget. It will teach them unspeakable volumes about how to handle difficult situations and how to love and build up their future spouses.

THE BOTTOM LINE

Most of what we learn in life is not taught but caught, and your children will catch far more from you than you ever realize. Your example is the one they will follow in their futures, both consciously and unconsciously, as the physical, visible model for how to negotiate life God's way. One of your strongest influences for your children is to become the person of character, integrity, and positive outlook that you hope they will one day become. Being someone your kids look up to and want to be like is one of the greatest gifts you can give your children.

CHILDREN LIVE WHAT THEY LEARN

BY DOROTHY LAW NOLTE

If a child lives with criticism,
He learns to condemn.
If a child lives with hostility,
He learns violence.
If a child lives with ridicule,
He learns to be shy.
If a child lives with shame,
He learns to feel guilty.
If a child lives with encouragement,
He learns confidence.
If a child lives with praise,
He learns to appreciate.
If a child lives with fairness,
He learns justice.
If a child lives with security,
He learns faith.
If a child lives with approval,
He learns to like himself.
If a child lives with acceptance and friendship,
He learns to love the world.

Chapter Four

EARLY TRAINING IS ESSENTIAL

Show your kids that you can handle them without breaking a sweat.[1] —Dr. Charles Fay, *When Kids Leave You Speechless*

Some parents approach child training with a vendetta. I (Paul) know I did. We wanted to "right the wrongs" we experienced when we were children. Memories of childhood frustration, however, often create blind spots in our thinking.

Parents who grew up in a poor family become determined to indulge their children in all that they did not have themselves when they were young. When they do, however, they cannot understand why their children are turning out self-centered and unappreciative.

Parents who were never allowed to play or participate in social activities as a child may overindulge their children with sports and recreational activities. They may require few chores, if any, of their own children. Then they wonder why their kids are lazy, complain of being bored, and are preoccupied with their own personal gratification.

Adults who had parents who were too rigid and strict are often tempted to be too permissive with their own children, and then are confounded when their kids are disobedient and disrespectful. Parents who were never allowed to speak their mind as adolescents tend to explain every detail why they do things to their children. They also elicit their kids' input on every decision. Then they act surprised when their children grow into sassy, smart-mouthed teens who question their parents' every action and wear their parents down arguing over the smallest of issues.

When we try to right the wrongs of our pasts in these and other ways, we allow our children to make excuses for their behavior. We allow them to argue their way out of responsibility or evade facing the consequences of their actions. A child whose excuses are routinely accepted will develop a victim mentality, believing not only that they hold no accountability for anything they do, but also that it is easier to skirt issues through self-justification and denial rather than to tackle them head-on. They often end up going through life just getting by. They also tend to avoid real engagement with their careers or spouses rather than bearing down to do the things they need to do to be successful in life and keep their relationships whole.

It might seem a bit counterintuitive, but creating a carefree, comfortable life for our children is not the fast lane to success—nor is giving them all the advantages of the childhood we wish we'd had. That doesn't mean we can't be a blessing to our children, but it does mean we need to hold them accountable for their decisions and allow them to experience some of the consequences of those decisions. As human beings, we only seem to learn from challenges and by accepting responsibility to fix whatever our actions have broken. The value of a dollar is not learned by having readily available spending money, but through having limited finances, working to earn money for what we want, and managing well what little we have. (If only our governments could learn that!) Interpersonal conflict resolution is learned through being committed to friendships and other relationships—like that of a teacher or supervisor at a summer job—rather than having the easy fix of abandoning the relationship, changing classes, quitting the job, or having Mom or Dad intervene. Values aren't tested until our kids face real temptations to break them. Character is formed more in the crucibles of life than in the fantasies of our Disneylands. As odd as it may sound, making things easier on our kids does not necessarily make life better for them in the long run.

Of course, the other extreme isn't a solution either. We don't want our children overstressed by facing overwhelming challenge after overwhelming challenge. Again, God is a guide in this:

> *God is faithful, who will not allow you to be tempted beyond what you are able, but with the temptation will provide the way of escape also, so that you will be able to endure it* (1 Corinthians 10:13).

God's plan for the family is that it would be a place of growth and learning. Loving parents come together as one to raise children. (We firmly believe that God put man and woman into the family because every child should be double-teamed! If you are a single parent, you need to be all the more vigilant and consistent about things, but we also believe God will enable you in this, if you will continue to ask Him.) As compassionate guides, coaches, and stewards, parents control the environment of children in their initial years, gradually widening that circle of influence until they are released into the world, hopefully able to face any trial or temptation and prevail. What is wonderful is that in each of these widening circles are new challenges for our children to conquer and new temptations for our children to resist. There is no need to artificially create circumstances to test our children—learning opportunities come naturally and age-appropriately as we open up their worlds—they are all around us!

The surprising thing is, quite often our children's misbehavior or violation of boundaries catches us, well...by surprise! In the spur of the moment their mistake, misdeed, disobedience, or even open defiance catches us flat-footed and unprepared. We believe that this generally happens for one of five reasons:

1. The parents are deceived about their children's rebellion and fall prey to their manipulation.

2. They want to believe the best of their children, so they are more than willing to let them cast the blame elsewhere or shirk the responsibility.

3. They do not know who to believe in a dispute and literally do not know what to do, so they accept excuses and send the children off with a warning rather than holding them accountable.

4. They hate conflict, and they would rather accept an excuse than confront the children about something they have done.

5. They choose their own comfort over their children's needs. Because correctly disciplining their children would take them away from something they prefer to do or will make them feel uncomfortable, they let it slide without realizing doing so will make things worse down the road.

So what do we do? Well, there's the rub. Unless we know what we are going to do before the challenge, we usually fail to act as we should. We might try to cajole our children by restating the rule or giving the instructions again; we might try to bribe them with a treat or a favorite activity; we might get angry and yell; or we might try any other number of other reactions that tend to either reinforce the misdeed or, at the other extreme, terrorize the child!

However, if you have a few strategies for how to react when childish moments erupt or a boundary you have set for your child is violated, instead of reacting in anger, you can *rejoice!* Yes, you read that right. Your kid messed up, and here you are presented with an opportunity to teach him or her something! You have a plan, and now you get to put it into action! You have an opportunity to help your child become a better person! You are also going to get a moment of connection with your son or daughter that does not happen in the smooth sailing of day-to-day life. If you handle it right, at the end of it, your relationship with your child will be stronger, your child will be wiser, and you can look forward to opening their world of responsibility a little broader in the future. Your son or daughter is maturing right before your eyes! Mistakes teach valuable lessons.

Of course, mistakes can be costly as well, and that is why it is best for us to allow our kids to make mistakes when the stakes are low. Then we can use those situations to teach them so that later in life, when the stakes are higher, they can avoid the problems that come with poor decision making, selfish indulgence, or a lack of proper respect for authority. This will allow them to develop a strong foundation in childhood upon which to build toward their futures. We believe that foundation is built on five guiding principles—obedience, honor, trustworthiness, self-control, and life principles.

1. Obedience: This is the primary standard for life—every other standard depends upon this one. Children must learn to obey standards outside of themselves before they can obey internal standards based on something other than selfishness. But as important as this standard is, you are not asking for blind obedience. Through what you ask your children to obey, you are imparting essential ingredients for life—wisdom, understanding, and knowledge. Every task you ask your child to perform is a teaching experience, as is every time they disobey. This gives a whole new meaning to win-win experiences!

2. Honor: Children need to show the respect that is due to parents and all others who are in authority. When the Roman centurion approached Jesus concerning his ill servant, Christ volunteered to come to his home. The Roman

told Jesus that he knew that would not be necessary for as he commanded many men, so also Christ had authority and needed only speak the word to grant the healing. The Bible then says that Jesus "marveled" and stated that He had seen no greater faith in all of Israel, for this man knew how to honor authority. (See Matthew 8:5-10.) Imagine saying something to Jesus and having Him "marvel" at what you said!

3.   Trustworthiness: Truthfulness becomes integrity over time as well as paves the way for accepting responsibility for one's actions. Trust is not something anyone owes you. Trust is earned. It is earned by being truthful, and it is the mark of a man or woman of God. Truthfulness must be taught and emphasized in all of our child-training efforts.

4.   Self-control: Children should be able to instantly obey parents the first time we ask and should grow to form the good habits of carrying out chores and responsibilities on their own. They should also have the discipline of putting responsibilities before playtime, which helps develop emotional intelligence.

5.   Life principles: As our children mature, they should develop their own standards to govern their actions and attitudes based upon truth, love, and a sense of personal destiny. The non-optional spiritual laws that govern all of life and living are represented in the life principles given to us in the Bible. Children must be taught these principles and how to live in harmony with them.

So how do you turn disciplinary confrontations into these building blocks of character? You discipline on principle, not according to how you are feeling at that given moment. You keep in mind the character traits you want to instill and develop a plan of action unique to each child. That doesn't mean you show favoritism or bias, but you look for the masterpiece hidden within and determine what you need to do to bring it out.

Most parents tend to have serious conflict with children when the child senses that the parents don't understand them. We need to remember that our children have different attributes, different skills, different personalities, different physical abilities, features, etc.—all by design of the Master Artist. We need to train our children in the way *they* should go—according to the design of the masterpiece God has created *them* to be—not necessarily in the way *we* think they should go.

To do that, there are some basic, somewhat universal questions you should consider as you make up your discipline plans for each of your children. Once you have answered these for yourself, you will be well on your way to rejoicing over learning opportunities rather than reacting in horror to what your "little monster" has managed to do now!

First, we must remember that we are *training up* our children, not just raising them. *Raising* means providing food and sustenance—it is maintaining life and fostering physical growth. That is an important thing to do, but it is not everything. We also have to *train* our children. What is *training*? *Training* is a conscious, active effort to instruct, discipline, and model. Training is not a by-product of a good environment, a loving home, and great schools. Training does not happen by osmosis. No wild horse was ever tamed by being grouped together with trained horses. Though children are very different from wild horses (most of the time), no more can we expect our children to be trained simply by putting them in a good place with others who are well behaved.

There is a warped concept of individuality that says it is wrong to impose our values on anyone, even our children, but even the experts are turning on that line of thinking now. Children are not born with an innate sense of goodness that is corrupted by the morals of their parents. Instead, they are born as selfish beings who need to be taught morality, honor, and love so that they can be delivered of that selfishness and become who God created them to be. You can be sure of one thing: if we don't impose our values on our children, someone else will impose theirs on them—and it is much less likely those values will be the ones we value!

At the same time, how we do train our children also matters. How we discipline and relate to our children communicates as much, if not more, than what we say. Though you may never have thought about it this way before, one of the best guidelines for how to parent is the Golden Rule:

> *In everything, therefore, treat people the same way you want them to treat you* (Matthew 7:12).

Every interaction with our children is a chance to model correct behavior. How do we want them to treat us when they are angry with us? Then that is the way we should model treating them when we are angry with them.

Do you ever wonder how well you handle difficult situations? If so, look into the mirror of your kids. Chances are, they will react to tough situations in a very similar way to how you react to them when they have created a problem. It can be a painful realization, but it is no less true.

THE BOTTOM LINE

The purpose of training your children from an early age is to demonstrate love to them by setting and enforcing real, protective limits that will deliver them from carelessness, thoughtlessness, and foolishness. Setting such limits gives them a practical outline for how to interact with others, including you as their parents. It is to ensure their God-given potential is being realized and their sense of proper moral behavior is growing in the right direction. When a tree is a sapling, it is easily formed or bent with the right pressure in the right place consistently;

but when it is fully grown, the only thing that pressure will do is break the tree. That is why we see so many lives broken, because those individuals weren't properly trained when they were younger.

Never forget that we are ultimately after the heart of the child. Restraining a child is more than just training him to behave with good manners and acceptable social conduct. Modifying outward behavior alone will not change the will or the condition of the heart. Teaching a child acceptable social behavior without dealing with rebellion and your child's attitudes will lead to children who may behave well around adults, but are otherwise terrors with little self-control. When this happens, usually in the teen years, your child will step into outright defiance, rejecting those things imposed upon him or her rather than things taught. The result is that one morning the parents will wake up and find their "good" child has gone "bad." Restraint can never be seen as just a way to modify outward behavior with superior strength and authority; discipline is not complete until the child acknowledges what he or she did was wrong, accepts that standard enough to sincerely repent, and then is forgiven. That is the only acceptable path to reconciliation and future peace in the home.

NOTE

1.   Jim Fay and Charles Fay, Ph.D., *When Kids Leave You Speechless* (Golden, CO: Love and Logic Institute, Inc., 2000), xxvi.

Chapter Five

EDIFYING CORRECTION

All discipline for the moment seems not to be joyful, but sorrowful; yet to those who have been trained by it, afterwards it yields the peaceful fruit of righteousness. —HEBREWS 12:11

Now, while things are calm and your children aren't misbehaving (or maybe they are in their beds asleep and you finally have some time to yourself), think back over your childhood and how you were corrected and disciplined. What brought you the most shame? Which ways of correction made you more rebellious rather than more obedient? What attacked you as a person rather than showed you what you were doing was wrong? Were you ever disciplined for making simple mistakes or for a misunderstanding, or only for blatant acts of rebellion?

In each of those situations, consider how you would have liked to be disciplined and what you think would have been more effective. If you are honest with yourself, you probably don't wish you had gotten away with things, only that you had been disciplined in a more loving and instructive way. Would you have preferred it hadn't happened in front of your friends or siblings? Do you wish your parents hadn't been so angry and out of control? Did yelling really work on you? Or was that just the first signal that your parents were serious about what they were saying? Did using your middle name work to get you to behave for the rest of the day? Or was there something else that worked better?

My (Billie's) dad only spanked me one time that I can remember. Believe me, it was well deserved. However, he had a bad habit of correcting me in front of company. This was very grievous to me as a child. It not only embarrassed me, but it made me angry. It made me think terrible things about him: that he was showing off, he was trying to prove he was tough, that he had so many things wrong with him, so why was he worried about the little things I did? Why did he correct me for this when I saw him do things he shouldn't do? Now, I know I was wrong in thinking these things, but I was a child who was hurt by her daddy. I needed understanding and correction *in private*, not in public. This type of discipline didn't help me. It didn't make me want to be better. It just made me mad!

Some of the times you were disciplined as a child may now give you stories to chuckle about during family gatherings, but at the time those situations weren't so comical. Most of the time we don't laugh because we got into trouble for something, but because we were so stupid to have pulled whatever stunt we did. Other times, when we think about it, even though it was years ago, it still stings. The hope is to make that different for our children by having a fair and balanced administration of justice in our homes. We want the lessons to stick more than anger over the punishment.

For all disobedience, rule breaking, and carelessness, there must be consequences, but one form of discipline does not fit all offenses. Careless mistakes have natural consequences, and as much as is appropriate for the age of the child, those consequences will teach invaluable lessons. A broken window from a baseball or softball has to be replaced. Your child can pay for that replacement out of his or her allowance, work extra chores around the house to earn extra money, and go to the store with you to purchase and then help install the window. If the child is older, he or she can help clean up the broken glass or even do the entire job while you supervise.

The great thing about letting natural consequences teach your children is that you can empathize with your children because you are on their side. They broke the window because they weren't being careful, so fixing the window is really their problem, and it is a problem they can handle. At the same time, because you love them and want them to learn from the experience, you will help them fix it. The more mature the children are, the more they cover the cost and participate in the replacement.

The other beautiful thing about letting consequences teach is that you don't even have to get angry about it. After all, we still do dumb things as adults—and do we get all that upset when we do? Think about how you feel when you make a mistake at work. If you make it on your own, you may get a little angry, but then you forgive yourself and fix the error. However, if your supervisor comes over and screams at you about the mistake, how do you feel then? Suddenly you are not as upset about the mistake as you are angry with the supervisor for "overreacting." The emotional outburst changes your focus from taking responsibility for the mistake to the "outrageous behavior" of your supervisor. Which do you learn more from? And which improves your relationship with your supervisor? Will you listen to that person more attentively in the future if they yell and scream at you, or if they feel bad with you but express their confidence that you are capable of fixing the mistake on your own?

On the other hand, what if you had just had a discussion with your child about not playing catch in the backyard? In that case, the window was broken because your child defied your instructions. Now you have two infractions: 1) the carelessness of breaking the window, and 2) a rebellious and disobedient attitude. In the first, once again, we can let the natural consequences teach a lesson, but rebellion is a different matter.

If there is one action of our children that violates all of our foundational principles—obedience, honor, trustworthiness, self-control, and forming good life principles—it is rebellion. Rebellion disobeys, disrespects, proves that your child can't be trusted to do what you asked or obey general rules, and shows the child is out of control. When children rebel, they are showing more of an allegiance to selfish desires than to positive life principles. In childhood, rebellion is the offense that deserves the severest penalty—something that lets your child know it will not be tolerated and is a big deal—and it also provides one of the greatest opportunities for you to teach your child a better way of life.

We want to teach our children to have qualities on the inside, not just to obey on the outside. That means that you don't tolerate rebellion whether it is open and in your face or is passive and subversive. Passive rebellion is a sour attitude, being withdrawn, sulking, pouting, or making others miserable because they are not getting their way. We want to teach our kids that they have control over their emotions, that they can choose how they act, even if they feel quite differently. They can be cheerful, even when they feel grumpy; or they can be respectful, even when they are angry. This is not being insincere; it is putting the best face on an unhappy or unfortunate situation. It is choosing to be respectful even when we don't want to be. It is choosing to live by principles rather than whim. This is an ability we should all have and need to develop in our children.

Be careful about reinforcing rebellion by ignoring it. Many strong-willed children have been reinforced in their rebellion by parents who only require obedience after:

1. repeated instruction,

2. an implied threat,

3. leaving the matter alone after they have asked repeatedly,

4. allowing children to argue about clear instructions,

5.   allowing the child to decide when he or she will finally obey,

6.   allowing children to habitually make excuses for disobedience or wrong-doing.

Solid boundaries can help curb or cure most of this kind of activity. Children should learn to obey immediately after the first time they are asked.

And if they don't? What if they act rebelliously and defiantly?

This brings us to one of the touchiest issues of parenting today. How do we discipline our children when they are rebellious?

Is It Okay to Spank Your Child?

In April 2010, the American Academy of Pediatrics posted the following statement on their website:

Children who are spanked at age three are more likely to be aggressive when they're five, even when you account for possible confounding factors and the child's level of aggression at age three.

Accordingly, their official stance on spanking is: "The American Academy of Pediatrics strongly opposes striking a child for any reason." They are not alone in this either. International pressure is growing against spanking, and even the United Nations Committee on the Rights of the Child issued a directive in 2006 calling corporal punishment "legalized violence against children" and urged nations to eliminate it in all settings through "legislative, administrative, social, and educational measures."

However, you don't have to look too far to discover that the research seems to lump together all forms of physically disciplining children as one. As one expert, Sandra Graham-Bermann, PhD, a psychology professor and principal investigator for the Child Violence and Trauma Laboratory at the University of Michigan, states, "It's a very controversial area even though the research is extremely telling and very clear and consistent about the negative effects on children.... People get frustrated and hit their kids. Maybe they don't see there are other options."[1]

When we speak of spanking a child and the biblical mandate that *"He who withholds his rod hates his son, but he who loves him disciplines him diligently"* (Prov. 13:24), we are not at all talking about striking a child in frustration or anger. *That is abuse, not discipline.* There are six different Scriptures in Proverbs that describe the importance of using a "rod" to discipline a child as an act of love, not an act of violence. It is to change behavior and get to the heart of the child, not to express your anger.

Some have tried to skirt the issue by saying the Bible doesn't tell us to spank our children, because the rod of correction in Proverbs is a "measuring rod," meaning we must have a standard of accountability for our children to live up to. That, of course, is true, but we don't really believe that is what the Scriptures are saying. They are indeed talking about a rod that is used to spank a child.

So this brings us to a seeming inconsistency: is spanking "legalized violence against children" and thus something that should be avoided at all costs? Or is it really true that refusing to spank our children is an act of hatred toward them, and that *"The rod and reproof give wisdom"* (Prov. 29:15), which cannot be obtained in any other way? Can we love our kids and still spank them, or does love dictate that we should never strike them for any reason?

Before we answer that, let's first clearly distinguish the difference between spanking, as advocated in the Bible, and abuse. Please hear us clearly on this: we in no way believe the Bible advocates abusing children in any way, shape, or form. When Proverbs talks about the rod, it is talking about using the implement for correction and never for abuse. Never, ever, ever is child abuse or battering an acceptable form of discipline. Never, ever, ever should we strike a child in frustration or anger. Biblical spanking is done with an instrument—a rod—not a belt, a hand, or anything else. Parents' hands are meant to hold and express affection for their children, not to strike them or punish them. Belts, paddles, or other devices can have undesired side effects, so the Bible advocates a rod or switch, not something harder and less forgiving or less controllable.

Correct spanking is a punishment *only* for open disobedience and rebellion—in other situations, natural circumstances and being held accountable will be all you need (with a little other engagement as well, as we will discuss shortly). It is done coolly, and the number of spankings should be in proportion to the offense. Spanking is to be done on the bottom only, no other place on the body, and should be done in such a way that, if the child should flinch, you will not strike the child anywhere else on the body. We believe God put natural padding there with this in mind—that the child would feel the sting of disobedience, but not be injured by it.

We also hold that spankings should not be given in front of others, but in private. The parent needs to have the child's full attention to explain why this punishment is being given. The parent should explain that he or she loves the child enough to do this, so that they will understand the importance of obedience and respect. Then afterward, the parent should love on them and be ready to forgive the repentant child. (If the child is not repentant, you will need to evaluate if he or she needs more time to think about it, if the child needs a further talking to, or if he or she needs to be disciplined again or in some other way.) When this process is finished, then the infraction is put into the past and there is no need to ever speak of it again. Each new act of disobedience is unique. Infractions of the past that have been dealt with and forgiven should not be brought up again, just as God doesn't bring up our offenses again once He has forgiven us.

Note as well that the Proverb says, *"The rod and reproof give wisdom"* (Prov. 29:15, emphasis added), not *"the rod of reproof"* as many misquote it. *Reproof* is verbal correction. It means that there will be discussion. You and your child need to talk about what happened and why. Furthermore, the discipline is not over until the parent and the child are reconciled to one another. Spankings alone do not correct—you need to be able to talk the situation through. Crying flushes out a child's guilt and clears the conscience; talking afterward restores the relationship and locks the lesson into the heart.

If you are in control of yourself when you discipline your child, you can teach your children to be in control of themselves when they face difficulties. If you are frustrated when you discipline them, then you create frustration in them. If you are angry, then you are just going to make them angry. This is what the research against physical punishment is showing: that overall, children who are punished by frustrated, angry parents become frustrated and angry themselves. That is why they are more likely to use physical *violence* to solve their problems at school, because that is what their parents modeled to them. Biblical spanking is quite another thing entirely.

So we need to discipline in the right way. There must be careful explanation, instruction, and reaffirming of your love, or the discipline will be misunderstood by the child. To do this, remember these three steps:

1.   Tell
2.   Teach
3.   Train

Tell your child what is right or wrong. You can't expect your children to obey unless you tell them what is acceptable and what they did that was rebellious. Help the child develop a set of core values. At first they will be external rules, until the child matures enough to internalize the concepts. As they grow older, your child will learn to make wise and right choices for him or herself. In other words, your child needs to learn to live within limitations and obey rules until he or she learns to live by the Golden Rule and the Law of Love.

When children see you angry, they harden for battle. When they see your grief over the offense, you are appealing to their consciences and touching their hearts. This, again, is why you must never chasten in anger. Maintain your judicial posture by showing grief over the offense making it clear that you are not disappointed in the child as a person, but rather you are grieved that he or she has chosen this act of disobedience against you, God, and him or herself.

Teach your children with words, attitudes, and your composure. Consistent repetition is an incredibly effective teacher. As children, neither of us were ever quite able to connect love with a spanking because, as far as we could tell, our parents never thought of it in those terms. You can help your child make this connection, though, by saying something like this:

> These actions (or this attitude) are wrong and as your parent, I cannot allow them to continue. Therefore, as a parent who loves you very much, I must discipline you properly to make sure this does not happen again.

Train your child to respond to your voice when it is calm. Don't teach your children to wait until you are ready to explode before they obey. Say it one time, in a conversational voice. Repeated warnings and threats only weaken your authority and encourage disobedience. Kids learn quickly when you do this that it is not what you say that matters—because you will say it again in just a few minutes. The previous request meant nothing—it's what you *do* that matters. Don't let that process stretch out, because it will only get worse. (We will discuss this more in detail in an upcoming chapter.)

After a discipline session, give children a few moments to cry and collect themselves, then take them in your arms. Don't force it. This will assure them of your love and forgiveness. It also allows you to assess the openness of their spirit—unwillingness to let you hold them indicates deeper issues and a possible closed heart, which you will need to address in a different way. In other words, your discipline session is not over yet. Remember that the goal is repentance, not punishment, so until that is achieved, you are not done.

If used correctly (there are exceptions depending on the child, of course), spankings should be uncommon. If we are consistent in our other parenting habits and continue to develop our relationship with our children, rebellion and disobedience should not be a norm. Kids will make mistakes, break things, and test limits, but none of those require discipline by spanking. They can be dealt with using more natural consequences, like extra chores, the loss of privileges, a heart-to-heart conversation, and other logical restrictions that have a wonderful way of presenting themselves at the time of the irresponsible act. (If they don't, there is no problem with saying that you will decide what is going to happen later. Give yourself time, if you need it. That has a tendency to make them think about it more, which isn't a bad thing either.)

WHAT IF WE DON'T WANT TO SPANK OUR KIDS?

Do you have to spank your children in order to have them turn out all right? Proverbs 23:13 tells us,

> *Do not hold back discipline from the child, although you strike him with the rod, he will not die.*

I think this was Solomon's way of trying to humorously say, "If you discipline your child, you are not going to kill him, even if he screams like he is dying. If you don't discipline him, however, when he is older, his lack of self-restraint just might! So which is better?"

The crux of the issue is that you have to have a way to discipline your children and bring them to repentance. Quite honestly, spanking is only one of many ways to do this, but at the same time it is simple, direct, and confined to a very specific, short amount of time. It is quick and to the point. You take them to their room or someplace private, speak with them, spank them, then love on them, and leave the room together, both the better for the experience.

Many times a spanking is better than grounding them from watching television or playing video games for a week, because it is over and done with rather than dragging on day after day and forcing you to deal with the perpetual "I'm bored," "What am I supposed to do?" and, "Can my punishment be over now?" Though it is good for our kids to be bored and figure out how to entertain themselves without video stimulation, you have to know you can withstand such a siege before disciplining in this way. If your children are so hooked on video stimulation in the first place, you may want to consider some new limitations!

At the same time, it is the repentance that is important. It is that the child learns a lesson that is the key, and there may be better solutions for your child than a spanking. For some children, a spanking may be no big deal. Certainly by the time your children are approaching adolescence, there are better ways to discipline them than by spanking. For teenagers, having their cell phone confiscated, their texting service blocked, or loss of car privileges, etc. are certainly more likely to get their attention while reinforcing the message every moment they are faced with the lost privilege.

Remember, as well, that discipline does not have to be done right away. If you are angry when the infraction happens, you should let yourself calm down before you do anything. There is nothing wrong with telling your child, "I am too upset about this right now to think clearly. We are going to talk about this later." Sometimes the dread of the coming discipline is worse than the punishment itself, which can help when you are later ready to calmly administer justice.

THE BOTTOM LINE

We established an understanding of discipline early on with Gretchen, Paul Edward, and Thom. Although we faltered from time to time, this was our normal procedure with our children:

1. When communicating with them, we would do so in a normal conversational tone of voice. We did not want to establish how seriously our instructions were to be taken by our volume.

2. We informed them only once, not twice or three times or more—only once. We didn't threaten, bribe, or reason with them. When we told them to do something, we expected them to do it when we told them the first and only time.

3. Consequences for not obeying—right away—were immediate and memorable.

Believe us when we say that just these three simple guidelines will change the atmosphere in your home. Training and consistent, loving discipline internalize self-control, wisdom, and the acceptance of responsibility. This will give your children valuable tools they will one day need to tackle the world's challenges. Loving discipline creates a bedrock for future success, just as it ensures a healthier family life.

NOTE

1. Brendan L. Smith, "The Case Against Spanking," the American Psychological Association website, http://www.apa.org/monitor/2012/04/spanking.aspx (accessed June 6, 2013).

Chapter Six

DISCIPLINE MEANS "TEACHING"

*A parent is a partner with God in making disciples
of their children.*[1] —DR. HENRY BRANDT

F ar too often when we think of the word *discipline*, we think of "pun-ishment." However, one of the root words of *discipline* is the word *disciple*, or as we would more likely say it today, *student* or *mentee*. Dis-ciples are people who follow a teacher, a coach, a craftsman, a mentor, a businessperson, a political leader, or someone they look up to in the hope of becoming more skilled, better educated, wiser, more capa-ble, and more adept at handling life. They become students of people who know more, who have found success for themselves, and who they would like to emulate in their own lives. Discipline is thus the process of helping disciples grow and learn. Though there can be some chastise-ment in that process to get the attention of the students and help them choose a better way, learning and growing is the goal, not punishing away bad behaviors.

To some degree or other, all of us are disciples of our parents. They have been our teachers and instructors, counselors and advisors, coaches and consultants. A coach is actually a good example of what parents do. Sometimes coaches have tough words or tasks for their players such as running laps or sprints, lifting weights, or doing endurance drills. Seldom, however, are practices all about doing pushups for not paying attention or running lines because of poor performance or bad attitudes. Most of what happens when coaches and players interact is instruction and training. Coaches teach the skills players need to compete and run plays over and over again until the players know them in their sleep. Coaches also motivate, inspire toward greatness, and teach that hard work has true rewards. Some coaches yell a lot, but the best ones encourage and challenge their teams to new levels of achievement and success, pushing their limits to do more than they thought they could. Coaches teach how to be gracious in victory and in defeat. In this way, they teach their players skills they will need for success not only in the game they are playing, but also along the road of real life.

One of the primary roles of a parent is that of a coach; from teaching our kids to play by the rules, to training them through household chores, to helping them with their homework, we motivate, train, and discipline. Parents act as teachers, coaches, and consultants throughout the lives of their children. At the same time, parents do this with much more of a sense of relationship. We are joined in spirit with our children more than any other adult will ever be.

We believe that to be successful parents, you need to:

1. know your child,

2. love your child,

3. train your child, and

4. discipline your child.

While we have discussed the last two already (and will more in the pages to follow), the first two are not emphasized enough in most teaching about parenting. This is perhaps because it is assumed that those are the aspects of parenting that most of us will naturally do, but we must never forget how important they are. We can never properly train and discipline if we do not know our children for who God created them to be and love them unconditionally.

So much of parental education focuses on the "crisis management" side of parent-child interactions—"How do we get our children to behave?" "How can we have a more peaceful home?" "How can we raise kids who make us proud?"—but the responsibility of parents to *disciple* their children is more a process of getting to know them, learning the God-given gifts put within them, and helping them develop into the blessings they are to be to the world (and to our families). In other words, it's really about how we perceive our children—it's about how we support who they are becoming.

No one can know your children like you can—nor can anyone correctly advocate for them as well as you, balancing their responsibilities, instilling virtues, and revealing the unique qualities that they have. Funny, too, that when you get to know them and spend the time to really listen to them, how much more smoothly other things go. It won't guarantee they will always behave correctly and intelligently (brain blips still happen!), but each time you openly listen to your children in non-confrontational encounters, you will make deposits in their emotional bank accounts that will give you quicker access to their hearts during tougher conversations.

SHOOTING FOR THE BULL'S-EYE

What is the aim as we disciple our children? We want them to grow up into a maturity that can help them handle whatever life throws their way. Maturity contains three main attributes:

1. Self-control
2. Wisdom
3. Responsibility

Having self-control means our children are not overpowered by their passions, emotions, desires, wishes, or curiosity—it doesn't mean they don't have these, only that they are not controlled by them. It means their passions, emotions, desires, wishes, and curiosity act as "advisors" to their decision-making processes, but none of them dominate rational, logical, moral, compassionate evaluation of what is the right thing to do. Many people think that true freedom is the ability to "do whatever one feels like doing," but when we are ruled by something other than our cognitive decision making and moral compass, we are not truly free. Self-control is what gives us the ability to choose to do what is right. That ability to choose fosters the selflessness necessary to live by love rather than obsessions, emotions, and in reaction to things that have hurt us.

Wisdom is a continuum of understanding, insight, ability to learn from experience, to make sound decisions, and to handle stressful issues with a level head. We have often heard it said that knowledge helps us understand what we face, but it is wisdom that helps us know what to do about it. With wisdom comes composure in the midst of stress and times of trial. This means that wisdom is built on a foundation of confidence and creative problem solving. Wisdom and self-control work together to create emotional intelligence—the ability to delay gratification until after our most difficult tasks are completed. All of these are invaluable in the pursuit of success in life.

The third component is the ability to accept responsibility. That's accepting personal accountability for one's own actions, but also the ability to step in and offer solutions for larger problems even if someone else caused them. Taking responsibility is the bedrock of faithful and conscientious work habits. Jesus is the ultimate example of stepping in to solve a problem—sin—that He didn't cause. Without responsibility, there is no integrity and reliability. This is also built on self-control and is tempered by wisdom.

Though there are many other attributes that we would like to have in our lives, these three define the maturity that allows us to develop intimacy with our spouses, be valuable employees in our workplaces, and to be contributing, respected citizens in our communities and churches. If this maturity is in our lives, it will help us solve the problems that we face and resolve relationship issues with others. It is the basis for good decision making and a source of strength for tough times and situations. More than good grades, school awards, championship sports teams, or whatever else most parents micromanage their children toward, instilling these three attributes into your children is going to help them be successful in life.

APPEASEMENT, BADGERING, MANIPULATION, OR DISCIPLINE?

As we have said before, each of your children is unique, and though you may have some similarities with other parents, your parenting style will be unique as well, a reflection of your personality, sense of humor, and the values you hold most dear. Believe it or not, from the time you first hold your child in your arms, your child has one major subject of study—you. Much of this study happens in the unconscious brain, but is extremely intricate and detailed. Without even thinking, as your children grow, they learn that when you do this or that, and they respond in this or that way, there tends to be a similar, predictable outcome. This condition is a two-way street, and the toddler brain can be a mastermind of diabolical manipulation if we neglect to be more conscious of the process than our children are. If you don't believe me, go to a playground or walk the aisles at the supermarket and look for the young mother or father frazzled from trying to keep up with their two-year-old. It is a sight you don't have to see twice to want to make sure it never happens to you.

The other side of the coin is that we parents have a distinct advantage in this process, if we would but use it. We can make our adult minds conscious of what is going on, and then watch and learn from it ourselves. While our youngsters are motivated by appetites, pains, desires, and emotions, we can be controlled by our intellects. This doesn't mean we will play a manipulative game of outsmarting our kids, but it does mean we can choose consistent, loving, edifying, and nurturing behaviors to inspire the same in our children. Remember, we are their number one and most interesting subject of study, so how we act and react matters greatly to our kids. If we proactively choose to behave responsibly before them and refuse to reward improper behaviors, then it won't take them long to experiment with new tactics to see if they can meet their needs and desires in a different—hopefully better—way.

Of course, this isn't a clear-cut process. Our kids aren't pigeons in a Skinner box—nor would we ever want them to be. Part of the mastermind motivation of children is that they want the maximum reward for the minimum effort. They will routinely experiment with shortcuts and disobedience, because it is often easier than virtue—if we parents let it be. If we allow them, those kinds of behaviors will be reinforced; but if we don't, our kids can quickly learn the benefits of being grateful, polite, and moral. Then those will become habits that last them a lifetime.

This is one area where starting with the negatives can make this easier to understand, even though we usually like to emphasize the positives. Here is a short list of two of our "favorite" examples of incorrect training—methods that are guaranteed not only to fail, but also to drive you crazy in the process:

1. Repeated threats and instructions.

2. Bribing/threatening/appeasing your children into obedience.

If a child can obey after the tenth time you have told them to do something, then that same child can obey after the first. When you repeat your instructions, you are reinforcing the response of the child to each of the previous times you asked—disobedience. If you do this often enough, your little mastermind student of parent nature learns a valuable lesson, "When Mom or Dad asks me to do something, they don't really mean it. In fact, they aren't really serious about it until (fill in the blank)." They will know within a couple of times of you repeating instructions that you don't really mean it until:

1. You start yelling.

2. You use their middle name.

3. You run through every child's name in your home (and sometimes the dog and cat) ending, in exasperation, with their name.

4. Your eyes begin to bulge and your face becomes the color of a tomato.

5. You begin the next sentence with something like:

    ✐ "I mean it!"

    ✐ "Now you've done it! Are you happy? You've pushed me over the edge!" (Trying to place the blame on them for your anger.)

    ✐ "If I have to come in there..."

    ✐ "Just wait till your father gets home!"

By the time you get to this point, you are exasperated, angry, and no longer thinking straight. And whose fault is that? While you may be thinking, "Look what you made me do now!" the truth is, it is not about what your child did in disobeying you that got you so upset, because if it was, you would have been upset after you first asked and he or she ignored you. No, it is your refusal to act after the first disobedience that has you so upset. Had you done something about it then, not only would you never have gotten angry, but your child would have learned:

1.   It is important to obey the first time, and

2.   My mom (dad) can handle me without so much as break-
     ing a sweat! They must love me enough to help me be a
     better person by training me up in the way I should go!

Of course the little masterminds in their head will never admit that.
Instead, they will just log it away for next time to either test the strength
of your resolve by trying the same thing again or look for a better way
to get what they want. Within these masterminds, however, patterns
are established quickly, so the name of the game is consistency. Chances
are, you won't get tested more than twice over any one issue or behavior.

How can you tell if you are in the habit of repeating instructions?
You hear yourself say something like, "I've told you a hundred times!" or
"How many times must I tell you?!" or "I'm not going to tell you again!"
But the truth is, oh yes you are! And your children know it! They know
when you are going to break! They see your eyes widening; they see the
foam at the corner of your mouth; they see your ears turning red. The
little mastermind within knows where your breaking point is and just
when to get out of the way!

If you hear yourself saying things like this, you have conditioned
your children to respond only when you are about to explode, not to
your request. Every time you repeat instructions, you are only giving
warnings. With every warning, your words carry less weight. "I've told
you a hundred times!" you say—well, they know you are willing to tell
them several more! They have learned that what you say is meaningless.
You have lost the respect necessary for successful training. Thankfully,
though, by changing your behavior, you can get it back very quickly.

When our children were very young—Tommy was around a year old
and Gretchen was probably five or six—I (Billie) used to make tapes of
the kids and send them to Paul, because he was on the road. I would
tell him things like, "Oh, your kids are speaking now and they're walking!" I would teach the children Scriptures to repeat and I would sing

songs with them. When the kids got married, I pulled some of the old tapes out and sent copies to the kids as mementos of their childhood. Gretchen and I were listening to one of them one time where I was teaching the two older children a song. I kept telling Tommy over and over again, "Put the shoes back, honey. Put them in the closet." Then we would return to learning the song and eventually I would again say, "Tommy, put the shoes back, honey. Put them in the closet." Finally, Gretchen said, "Mother, why didn't you do something about that! I can't believe you kept telling him over and over again! How many times have you warned us about doing that with our kids?" We both got a pretty good laugh out of that! I thank God that we eventually learned this lesson and changed our behavior.

Another thing we shouldn't do is threaten our children. For example, avoid saying such things as:

- "If you don't do _____, you are going to be in big trouble."

- "Want me to get the spanking rod? Here I go!" Stomp, stomp, stomp down the hall. "Okay, I am getting the rod! Now I've got it! And I'm coming in now to give you a spanking, if you haven't obeyed yet!" or

- "One...two...two and a half...two and three quarters..."

Or you blatantly lie to your kids with something like, "If you don't behave yourselves, we're going to leave you here at Disneyland. They will chain you into 'It's a Small World' and you will be there forever, singing that song, over and over and over again!" That may give you a chuckle, but we've heard parents say things like that!

Never make statements to your children about consequences you would never follow through on. It just depreciates your word—and what will you do if they call your bluff? Which, of course, those little masterminds will eventually figure out to do.

You should also never bribe for obedience with statements such as:

- "If you sit still in the grocery cart, I'll get you a treat when we check out."

- "If you will get into your bed for your nap, I will read you your favorite story."

- "You may have cake for dessert, if you eat your vegetables."

Threatening, trying to placate, or offering rewards for better behavior takes the responsibility to think and act correctly out of the children's hands and places it in yours. Now they are no longer responsible for their behavior—you are! It also tells them that they only have to behave when rewarded. However, if you instead take them aside to discipline them after the first instruction to stop, tell them what they did and why it is unacceptable, then you have placed the responsibility back on their shoulders. They will think differently about it next time and they will understand that obeying the first time is the way to go.

Of course, there are often extenuating circumstances for how your children are behaving—they may be tired and cranky, they may have just been to a birthday party and had too much sugar, or whatever else might be affecting them—but you have to resist the urge to make excuses and let the behavior slide. If you do, you will pay for it double down the road! Teach your children that they are capable, self-controlled human beings by acknowledging that despite extenuating circumstances, they are still in charge of their own behavior. They can still choose to do the right thing. Ethics are not situational or subject to how we feel at the moment.

Now, this doesn't mean you can't reward your children if they are good, but just don't make it conditional on them behaving well in the first place. You reward them because you love them and you are a good parent. When you bribe them, it sets up the expectation that they don't have to behave unless there is some kind of reward promised. Instead, obedience should always be expected—rewards are just fun perks of them being your kid, because you are a fun parent!

Another way parents often choose to manipulate their children to do what they want is to withhold love and affirmation. In short, the parent pouts, teaching the child that their love and approval is based on what the child does or doesn't do. When this happens, kids get mixed signals. They don't get the message, "I misbehaved, but I am really better than that because my parents love me no matter what. I am capable of doing better!" Instead, the line of thinking goes something like this: "I do bad things because I am a bad kid. I am so bad, in fact, my parents don't even like me anymore." To withdraw your love and approval when children disobey constitutes emotional abuse and is a totally inappropriate response. It forces children to comply in order to earn your love rather than want to please you because they know you love them no matter what. This is more than crucial when they get older and their thinking is less black and white, and times of discipline demand more explanation and discussion.

How do we know these things are problematic? Yes, we admit it: we learned from experience. We messed up in these areas, but gradually learned to do better as we got to our third child. We saw these principles work even better as we taught them to our kids when they became parents, and we practice these principles as grandparents. It was toughest with our oldest, of course. I (Paul) remember one time telling Gretchen, "You just have to forgive Dad. I have never raised children before. This is the first time I have ever done this."

Naturally, she responded, "Well, Dad, you'll have to forgive me—I have never raised a daddy before, either."

If you are able to resist such reinforcements of negative behaviors when your children are young, you will find that as they get older, discipline becomes more about instruction than about punishment. If your children are older when you learned this, you can still change things. It will just take more consistency and resolve. Either way, remember it is not so much about what your children do as it is about what you do. Determine you will discipline without anger; you will make sure a lesson is learned, not just that the child is punished; you will love them all the way through; and you will forgive them when they repent of what they did. Then, just as God does, we can throw the transgression into the sea of forgetfulness and go back to nurturing, enjoying, and loving, being the parents of the gifts God has given us in our children.

THE BOTTOM LINE

Discipline is a planned action of love. Abuse is a reaction of anger; it is the venting of parental frustration and perpetrates violence on children causing them to act violently toward others. Young ones raised with loving chastisement are typically the least violent among children, because they are self-restrained. They are not ruled by their anger or other explosive emotions and have been trained to behave kindly and with respect.

Chastisement should be done after the first offense while the parent is calm. Abuse results when parents do not bring swift chastisement, but instead wait for the child's continued rebellion to make them angry enough to respond. Punitive discipline is incorrectly used if it is a last resort rather than a first response. Chastisement is loving and constructive; abuse is hurtful, demeaning, uses verbal attacks aimed at our children's hearts and identity. Chastisement draws a parent and child together. Abuse alienates and separates.

Consistent discipline brings your children up in training and instruction toward maturity. It teaches them the importance of acting with self-control, seeking wisdom, and taking responsibility to be part of the solution in any situation. When your children possess these attributes, they are not tripped up by emotional baggage, and their gifts can be more easily released. They will get along better with others, have the emotional intelligence to put work before play and the needs of others before their own, and they will have the freedom to be who they were created to be, not hampered by selfishness or bad habits. Consistency is also the key to emphasizing the instructional side of discipline. When you do it right, you not only help your child grow toward success, but you also create a relationship with them that will last a lifetime.

NOTE

1.   Henry R. Brandt, *Build a Happy Home with Discipline* (Wheaton, IL: Scripture Press, Inc., 1960), 2, in Charles R. Swindoll, *You and Your Child* (New York: Bantam Books, 1980), 85.

Chapter Seven

UNDERSTANDING THE SPIRIT OF YOUR CHILD

*Rules without relationships will always lead
to rebellion.*[1] —JOSH MCDOWELL

The spirit of a person is what we sometimes call the heart. It's the innermost being of that individual. As Proverbs 4:23 tells us, *"Everything you do flows from it"* (NIV). The spirit is the very essence of our being. It is not the soul, which is made up of the mind, will, and emotions.[2] It's who we really are, what we really feel even beyond the emotions of the soul. The word in the Hebrew for *spirit* also translates as "breath." It could be described as our life energy, because our spirits are what make our bodies alive.

Our children's spirits are really tiny gold mines with one critical difference. The more gold you take out of a gold mine, the less there is left in the mine. However, with our children, the more you mine the gold God has deposited into their spirits, the more gold there is to find. Our children are thus treasures in fleshly vessels. From before the time they were born, God hid within them talents, interests, physical and intellectual abilities, all of the fruit of the spirit in seed form, giftings, passions, and other treasures that are there for us as parents to draw out. All of these are clues to your child's calling in life and the purpose God has placed in them. Some ministers refer to this as the way that God has "bent" our children—that they have divine leanings or tendencies to go in the direction God wants them to go. It is also within their spirits that they feel the need for divine nourishment—a magnetic impulse that draws them toward God. It is the "way in which they should go" as mentioned in Proverbs 22:6, or, as it says in the Amplified Bible translation of this Scripture:

> *Train up a child in the way he should go [and in keeping with his individual gift or bent], and when he is old he will not depart from it.*

We are to discover and uncover these gifts in our children, discern the way they are "bent" by God for His glory, and then raise them up in a way honoring those predispositions and callings. We are not to make of our children what we think they should be, but who God planned them to be.

Thus, if you want your training to be godly and effective, observe your children, talk with them, and recognize the way in which they are each individually bent. Be sensitive and alert so that you will discover God's roadmap for their lives that He hid within them and then adapt your training accordingly. Recognize them as the gifts they are to the world. Train them in the way they should go.

Now some of this training will be very generic. Morality, God's Word, proper etiquette, respect for authority, wisdom, and such overarching principles are important for every child. They are the backbone of proper social interaction and oil the gears of success in the various realms of life. Every child needs schooling, exposure to sports, music, or other activities, to be encouraged to read widely, allowed to express themselves artistically, and to be given adequate free time to investigate subjects or hobbies that interest them for themselves. God doesn't write the "bents" of our children on the backs of their hands, but on their hearts, and we have to facilitate them being revealed to ourselves, our children, and the world.

Other things, as our children grow, will be very specific. Some of the things our kids want to pursue will be rabbit trails that eventually come to nothing. Others will grow in size and dimensions like a stream flowing into a river. Some might begin when our children are very young; others won't appear until late adolescence or early adulthood. They are there, however, and it is a big part of our job as parents to recognize them and help cultivate them. We can't be pushy, however, as they must also be embraced by our kids for them to develop. Too often children are almost force-fed such things by their parents and the kids burn out on them before they have a chance to really embrace their bents for themselves. When that happens, it can take years for kids to get back to where God wanted them from day one. We are guides, consultants, and coaches in this process, not dictators.

We need to be very careful as well about mistaking our own passions and interests for those of our children. Dads who were the football hero in high school can get too excited about their son getting a scholarship to play college ball, or moms who never got the chance to take dance lessons when they were young can obsess over their daughter becoming a ballerina. There is certainly nothing wrong with sharing these interests with our kids, passing on what we know, and encouraging them to participate in things we like to do, but we have to be careful about replacing what God has called them to do with what we are calling them to do. We can't mistake a shared interest as a lifetime pursuit. It's not about us, after all, but about our kids, their relationship to God, and their happiness that is wrapped up in them fulfilling their own destiny. There is nothing wrong with pushing our kids toward things we are interested in, even though they may not completely share those interests at first, but we just can't let them become a misplaced obsession. We have to balance that with what our kids are choosing for themselves.

It is wonderful for us to want our kids to succeed and have all the advantages of good grades, the best classes, and championship performances, but these desires are behind a trend that is all too prevalent today, and that is micromanaging our kids to look the part of success, but not really have the character or fiber of it. This means we make sure our kids look good, perform well, get the right grades, are on the right teams and in the right clubs, and get into all of the honors classes, but none of these are things they have chosen or earned for themselves. In fact, these kids tend to have had all of their choices made for them by their parents and rarely if ever have had to experience the consequences of their own actions. These are the kids who march out of high school looking like they have the world by the tail, but then flunk out of their first year of college because they can't function on their own. They have no idea how to balance the "fun and freedom" of college life with the things they need to do to succeed away from Mom and Dad.

Unfortunately, it is something you see every fall at colleges across the US. People scratch their heads and wonder what happened to these kids who seemed model students, athletes, and citizens in high school, but they failed to fly because there was very little character or work ethic behind the façades. Their "success" had much more to do with what Mom and Dad were doing behind the scenes than the people they were becoming as they were growing up.

While discerning our children's gifts and callings takes focus and attention, it is also one of the greatest joys of parenting. When we see our kids succeed at something they have chosen to do and pursue for themselves, our chests swell with pride and we experience what is likely the same pleasure God feels when we step into all He has planned for us to be. We can't imagine any greater reward as parents—or as grandparents!

COMMUNICATION OPENS THE DOOR TO YOUR CHILD'S HEART

There are six things to remember when you are talking with your children to make the communication both meaningful and relationship enhancing. Remember:

1) Use your eyes.

Eye contact is crucial, not only when you are communicating with a child, but in fulfilling the child's emotional needs. Without realizing it, eye contact is one of the primary ways that we convey love and respect. This is especially true with children. The child uses eye contact with his parents and others to feed emotionally. Remember how the infant learns from the distance of the parent's face to where the baby's face is as the child is held? Most of this interaction comes through the eyes. The more parents make eye contact with their child as a means of expressing their love, the more the child is nourished with affection, and the fuller the child's emotional tank will be. So when you talk with your children, convey your love for them through looking at them eye to eye.

2) Use your heart.

Love your children for who they are. Do you enjoy being your child's mom or dad? Have you taken time to thank God for these wonderful gifts you call your children? Do you communicate to them how important they are to your life? This is done with words as well as actions, but those words must come from your heart. Books that have blessings and encouraging things to say to your children can be a help if you are at a loss for how to begin, but once you get more practice, don't just quote rote blessings and Scriptures, but let your heart lead you to the right words to speak over each of your children. Let each word be filled with meaning from your heart.

3) Use your ears.

The greatest communication tool God created is not your mouth; it's your ears. "*He who gives an answer before he hears, it is folly and shame to him*" (Prov. 18:13). I (Paul) have to admit that this wasn't something I was very good at when our kids were small—or even when they were teens, really. I always spoke before I listened. I thank God that I am a much better listener today for my grandkids—and even for our children.

It is important to note here that listening to and trying to understand the ideas of your children is not the same as endorsing those ideas or agreeing with their reasoning. Instead, listening gives you an invaluable opportunity to know exactly what your child is thinking, and an even more valuable opportunity to suggest other rational options to them—*once you have let them have their say*. Seek first to understand, then to be understood. In this, you also teach your children how to handle difficult conversations—a lesson that will be useful for their entire lives.

How do you let your children speak their mind? By listening, listening, listening. Allow them to have their own opinions about things. If they are wrong, respectfully explain why you believe differently. But if they are within the realm of tolerance—in other words, it doesn't violate a biblical standard—then they are entitled to their own opinion. This is part of them becoming the confident, educated, rational adults you want them to be.

Say, for example, as a teenager one of your kids is dating a boy or a girl who you don't want them involved with. To attack the faults and drawbacks of that boy or girl isn't the best approach. Instead, address the way your child is thinking and find out why they are drawn to that person. Once you have listened to understand, then try to explain your vantage point and why you think your child is not seeing things correctly. Give your teen something to think about rather than a list of shortcomings that could be seen as attacks. Your teen has to decide, not you; but if you listen and give solid advice, most of the time your child will come to the right conclusion.

Allow your children to have their own thoughts, their own ideas, and their own opinions about things. A prohibition against rebellion is not a prohibition against thinking for one's self. Challenging the way you think is not rebellion. It is part of the process of deciding things for themselves. In fact, it is really just a roundabout way of asking what you really believe. If you can clearly explain and show why you believe what you believe, then they will often accept that once they understand it for themselves.

We made the mistake of never allowing our children to have their own opinion. We think that is a counterproductive thing, because ultimately we want them to learn to think for themselves. If they don't know why they believe the things they do, it isn't all that difficult for some clever college professor or charming coed to talk them out of it. We need to help our kids develop their minds and grow intellectually.

It's also amazing how we will spend more time and be more patient and compassionate with other people's children than we are with our own. That's a big mistake. We need to give our own kids every advantage and consideration we would give someone else's child. This isn't a natural tendency, though. We need to realize that this happens and make the extra effort to let our kids speak their minds and hearts to us.

When Gretchen was older, I (Billie) asked her what she would have changed about the way she was raised. She said, "I wish you would have taken time to understand me, not to have just been a mother all of the time." I realized that I had made the mistake of thinking if I'd given them a chance to express ideas that I didn't agree with, they wouldn't learn to think the same way that Paul and I did. I felt if I could keep them from saying it, I could keep them from thinking it—but then, of course, the very opposite is true. Because I didn't listen to their ideas, however offensive those ideas might have been to me, I never gave myself the opportunity to explain why we thought the way we did. I missed the opportunity to teach them the logic of the truths we hold dear and the reason for the opinions we have.

I didn't realize that one of the greatest ways we communicate acceptance of our children for who they are is by listening to them. And of course, accepting them doesn't mean we accept every idea that comes through their head—but accepting them does allow us to discuss those ideas in an open and loving way.

How much time do you spend talking *with*—and not just *to*—your children?

4) *Use your words.*

Children regularly need to hear that you love them, especially when they have misbehaved. They need to hear you say you are proud of them. (That, of course, you can save for times other than when they have misbehaved.) In every situation, there is always something positive that you can pull out. For every time you catch your child doing something wrong, make an effort to catch them doing something right—in fact, try to catch them doing something right several times more often. Always do what you can to communicate that you understand and value the masterpiece God created your child to be.

5) *Use your arms.*

Hugging your child, touching them on the shoulder, or taking their hand not only conveys that you love them, but that you are listening—that you want to connect, be present with them, and understand how they are feeling. Remember that you should never use your hands to strike your children or grab them roughly. Your hands and arms are there to embrace, give hugs, snuggle, and convey the warmth of your caring.

6) *Use your feet.*

Attend your child's ball games and activities, share their interests, and let them jabber excitedly about what they did in the car ride home after an event. Tell your children how proud you are of their efforts and dedication to their endeavors. If things don't go so well, take the opportunity to do something a little out of the routine afterward to talk about it and affirm that you love them no matter what. Let them know that games and such are more for what we learn from them than just about winning and losing. There are bigger challenges ahead in life. These experiences are preparing them for those times. Never let them forget that God has big plans for them.

THE BOTTOM LINE

Your child is a gift of God to you, but also to the world he or she touches. There are special gifts, talents, and interests that will develop as your child grows up that are all important clues to who he or she has been called to be. However, there is a big key to your children plugging in to that calling—namely, you as their parent. It is first in relationship to you that who they are is revealed, and then as they grow and mature, in their relationship to God and others.

You must never neglect the privilege of being your child's parent, nor should you ever belittle how blessed they are to have you as their parent. There are special gifts, talents, and interests in you as well that God has chosen to have in your children's lives. Don't neglect to share who you are even as you investigate to learn who they are becoming. So many wonderful things happen in the relationship space you create with your kids. Enjoy it and make it a priority—you will never regret the special times and memories that such a pursuit will make room for.

NOTES

1.   Josh McDowell, sermon at West Acres Baptist Church, Evans, Georgia, Fall 2009.

2.   We realize that some feel like the spirit and the soul are one entity and cannot be separated. However, the apostle Paul treated them as separate and distinct entities in First Thessalonians 5:23 as we have done here: *"Now may the God of peace Himself sanctify you entirely; and may your spirit and soul and body be preserved complete, without blame at the coming of our Lord Jesus Christ."* Hebrews 4:12 echoes this, telling us they are dividable, *"For the word of God is living and active and sharper than any two-edged sword, and piercing as far as the division of soul and spirit."*

Chapter Eight

GUARDING OUR CHILDREN'S HEARTS

A healthy spirit conquers adversity, but what can you do when the spirit is crushed? —PROVERBS 18:14 MSG

When a spirit is crushed or wounded, everything about a child is affected, especially his or her ability to communicate and interact with others. If our spirits are wounded, we withdraw into a self-protective mode and do everything we can to avoid further hurt or pain. Think of it as the breath being knocked out of you. Anyone who has participated in a sport knows how that feels. When that happens, we forget about everything but trying to get the next breath.

When we are dealing with children, a crushed spirit means the lines of communication shut down and all training stops. At this point, discipline often only deepens the problem and increases frustration on the part of parents and the child. To try to discipline your son or daughter now is like demanding that he or she run on a bruised or broken foot. Anytime discipline, especially chastening, fails to produce compliance, wise parents will stop and check on the current state of the spirit of their child.

When the spirit of a child, or any person for that matter, is hurt, wounded, or closed off, they get quiet and begin to withdraw emotionally and physically from the offending person. Normal conversation ceases, answers become evasive, and information is cryptic. Hurting children often avoid being touched, much less held or hugged. If embraces occur, they are perfunctory, at best. Spontaneous demonstrations of outward affection are nearly nonexistent. In short, something is wrong and the attentive parent can feel it in the air.

At this point, many parents just hope it will pass; and if the wounds are not too deep, if the child is somewhat mature, and if forgiveness is a normal practice in your family, it may indeed pass with time. However, when it doesn't, the child becomes more withdrawn, rebellion increases, and rejection of the parents by that child or teen becomes undeniable. Normally obedient children can suddenly launch into defiance in their attitudes and actions. Children who once enjoyed being around parents suddenly want to hole up in their rooms and be alone.

We fear that too many times actions like these on the part of adolescents have been accepted as a "phase" when in reality, it is the response from a crushed spirit. Failure to deal with and heal such wounds can affect the rest of a child's life.

CAUSES OF A CLOSED SPIRIT

Conflict, confrontation, hurt feelings, and pouty lips are all normal occurrences in many homes. Most of the time they occur without lasting impact or damage. However, there are things that go beyond the bumps and hiccups of everyday living and touch us down to our innermost beings. This is not a rap on the knuckles or pop on the noggin—it is a sucker punch to the mid-section. It is something that hurts so badly it lingers seemingly without end. A wounded spirit is an injury and not something you can just shrug off. A wounded spirit stops you in your tracks. It does so because the one who is in a position to wound your spirit is one to whom you have bestowed a great deal of love and trust. They are people to whom we are vulnerable, and when they hurt us, it cuts deeply.

Adults can choose the people who have such power in their lives; children cannot. So as parents, we are the first our children trust and give their hearts to without reserve. But alas, we make mistakes, and have issues of our own. Therefore, we must be sensitive as to how those mistakes and the hurts of our own pasts affect their little hearts. We must be ready to admit when we mess up, and we must be willing to go to our children for forgiveness.

The good news is that kids are the most forgiving and resilient creatures on earth. It's a pride-filled and irresponsible parent who fails to cherish the privilege of trust given them by their children. We should never be reluctant to ask for forgiveness from our children when we mess up concerning them or if we wound their spirit in any way.

Unjust Discipline

Unjust discipline is quick to wound the spirit of a child. Perhaps they were wrongly accused, did not understand the rule that was broken, or you realize afterward that the punishment was more severe than was warranted. Parents sometimes jump to conclusions and discipline in the heat of the moment, only to find out later they didn't have all of the facts. It happens. And when it does, we must stop and right the wrong, ask forgiveness, and repent of our error. Failure to do so can lead to a bruised spirit in our child. It is very difficult for our kids to trust and love someone who will not admit when they are wrong. God forbid that should be us!

Broken Promises

We live in a different world than our children. While we have so many different concerns and responsibilities, their world often revolves around ours. When we make promises, especially concerning time and activities with them, they must be seen as high priorities. A *broken promise* can crush a spirit. Though our world contains hundreds of voices calling for our attention, a child's world has relatively few, and our voices are the most precious to them. Promises are cherished alongside their most-prized possessions. If we get distracted, forget, or actually choose to place something above a promise to them, they feel it and feel it deeply. You are the first to hold their hearts in your hands; drop it by betraying their trust and it may be a long time before you get to hold it again.

Moral Inconsistencies

A third and very serious cause of a wounded spirit in children is *moral inconsistencies* in their parents. Some parents foolishly assume that if their children aren't aware of the undisciplined or morally impure areas of their lives, it doesn't hurt them. Whether it's some kind of impropriety, pornography, or adultery, or simply a lack of self-control manifested in an uncontrolled temper, profane language, or an overindulgence of alcohol, substance abuse, or even food, the ultimate end is the same: "*He who sows wickedness reaps trouble, and the rod of his fury will be destroyed*" (Prov. 22:8 NIV).

Recently someone shared the following example with us:

A young couple had their first son and he seemed to be incorrigible. The dad was a leader in his church, as had been his father before him. As a talented vocalist, he sometimes led worship and he and his wife were dedicated homeschool parents. Yet the child refused to respond to discipline or training. Both grandfathers actively participated in efforts to aid and reinforce discipline in the home from a distinctly biblical approach. Though there were moments of seeming breakthroughs, no lasting solutions were found. Then it happened, and everything became very clear. This dad was caught in adultery, which had been going on for some time.

Secret sin will always find us out.

An Unhealthy Marriage Environment

A fourth area that should be obvious, but bears mentioning, is an *unhealthy marriage environment* in the home. The list of reasons why a stressed marriage wounds children is long and distinguished. Parents must be of one accord if there is to be unity in the home. Otherwise, a child is often forced to choose one parent over another or is played between them because of their frustrations. As it is not our intent in this book to deal with marital issues, we urge you to get our book, *Get Married, Stay Married.* In it we tell our story of how our own challenges affected our family, and then things we did both to repair our marriage and heal our relationships.

Parental Rejection

Parental rejection or neglect is extremely damaging to a young heart. In fact, research indicates that neglect can cause more harm to the development of a child than overt physical abuse, especially for infants.[1] The lack of care in the first year severely inhibits development that is not easily caught up in later childhood. While this has largely been a question of care in foster homes and orphanages, it is also an issue with being unwanted after birth.

For older children, parents don't always understand what they have done that makes a child feel rejected. They can spend a lot of sleepless nights wondering what has happened to their normally compliant child or teen. As mentioned before, parents are the first people children trust with their hearts. When moms and dads do things that convey rejection to their children or actually reject them purposefully—and too many mistake rejection for a valid form of discipline—the spirit of the child can be deeply wounded.

There are basically two types of rejection that we need to be concerned with—overt or outward rejection and covert or inward, subtle, often accidental rejection. Overt rejection is open or obvious behavior that conveys the message that children are unwanted or unloved, and it is oftentimes done in anger. Telling children they are unwanted, that you wish they had never been born, that they are more trouble than they are worth, that they were unplanned, or that you really desired a child of the opposite sex, all constitute rejecting words and actions. Covert rejection is more subtle, but just as damaging. It often involves isolating the child from others or ignoring their needs and appeals for affection.

Overt rejection is often perceived by the child who is neglected when parents are too involved with their own lives (whether school, job, career, friends, or church) or the lives of other children inside or outside the family. Parenting extremes—whether a lack of love conveyed in the absence of restraints, or a lack of love expressed in overly strict, harsh, unloving restraints—convey rejection to children. Should a parent leave—whether due to a job or divorce—the child usually sees it as rejection. (This can include a military parent who is deployed for an extended time.) A mentally or physically handicapped child may feel rejected from all directions—family, friends, and God.

Covert rejection occurs in ways not easily seen or intended by parents. Overprotection to the point of isolationism, the refusal to allow children to mature by making decisions for themselves, or overindulgence to the point of not requiring responsibility for their actions are a couple of the most common mistakes parents make. Another very common covert rejection happens when love is withdrawn as punishment or discipline. This can happen when a negligent parent finally has all he or she can take of a child's behavior and then disciplines harshly in anger attacking the child's person instead of dealing with the behavior.

The death of a parent can also be perceived by surviving children as rejection. In one case, a daughter was unable to have normal sexual relations with her new husband, and the root of the problem was found to be feelings of rejection by her father who had died just a few weeks before their wedding. Adopted children sometimes have to deal with rejection and a closed spirit that runs all the way back to their birth parents, even in the presence of wonderful adoptive parents. There's always a question for orphans: "Why did my birth parents not want me?" Last, an only child sometimes has to deal with feelings of rejection, at times from overprotection or overindulgence, and at other times from neglect, or simply because they have no brothers and sisters as do other children and so feel isolated and alone.

As you can see, it is not always a parent's fault when the spirit of a child closes from feelings of rejection. When it does, whether or not the parent is at fault doesn't really matter. The end result is the same. The parent is in danger of losing their ability and privilege to parent their children successfully. So we must be sensitive to the symptoms of a closed or bruised spirit in our children and work to keep that spirit open when it is wounded. Think of it as keeping them healthy and in shape for the game of life. What is important is that we realize the presence of rejection and move to deal with and resolve it.

REOPENING YOUR CHILD'S HEART

Reopening your child's spirit is done most effectively if you act in a timely and direct manner. Think of the child as being on the playing field of life. You are the coach on the sideline and you see your son or daughter down on the field, injured. Discipline, performance, and achievement are all on the back burner now. This child is injured and you must tend to his or her wounds before he or she can return to the game.

The first step is to express your empathy concerning the pain and your desire to listen and understand the source of that pain, even if that source is you or something that you have done. It may take time for the child to admit what is really on his or her mind, so you will have to be patient. A show of impatience often convinces the child of the futility of thinking that you might understand later. When the time comes, listen deeply to what your child is expressing, even if you think the child is wrong. You must hear the nearly "silent sounds of the soul" at this point. Remember that it is not necessarily what the child says, but what he or she really means to say. Ask probing questions to open up further insight and clarify anything you are not sure that you understand. Repeat back to the child what you are hearing until he or she confirms that you are on the right track. This assures the child that you are really listening and assures you that you understand what your child is communicating to you.

If the source of your child's pain is something you have done or said, you must acknowledge the offense from the child's perspective. If it was unintentional or unavoidable, a carefully thought out explanation may make a wonderful teaching time, but you must not make excuses or become defensive about what happened. Even if the child's perspective is skewed, it will stay skewed until you teach the child differently. Should you come to a place where the two of you just can't agree, you can agree to disagree and continue to show respect and honor to each other's perspective and feelings. Your genuine love and concern for your child's feelings and your treatment of him or her as a valued member of your family will determine how successful you are in re-establishing communication and respect.

A child's spirit is like a rose bud. Try to open it by force and you damage and destroy the beauty of the flower. Warmth and light opens a rose. You must nurture it open. So it is with your wounded child. Care and concern, understanding and love—these are the tools you must use to address a crushed spirit. When that spirit begins to open, you will know it because the child not only allows you to hug and cuddle him or her again, but welcomes it. This is a great sign that you are making progress.

Finally, if it is established that your child's spirit was closed because of something you did, you must ask forgiveness. Put your pride aside, ask for forgiveness and wait patiently for it to come. Get an answer. "Will you forgive me?" Wait for a response. If there is a refusal to forgive, then more work will need to be done and you may need to seek counsel from someone outside of your family whom you trust. If the child simply needs more time, then give the Holy Spirit time to work on your child's heart. Be sure to follow up later, though. The issue is still an open wound between you until forgiveness is granted. The child needs to express his or her forgiveness and you need to hear it. Remember, repentance and forgiveness are a lot alike—both are a work of God. Relax and give God time to heal your child's heart.

THE BOTTOM LINE

If we are going to expect our children to be open and honest with us from childhood and into young adult life, we need to be able to be open and honest with them, confessing when we hurt them and asking forgiveness. We need to be sensitive enough and discerning enough to also see when they have been hurt and their spirits may have been bruised or crushed. The greater the damage that has been done, the more patient we need to be in guiding them to healing.

Open communication with our child's heart is important for all aspects of parenting, most meaningfully, for the sharing of love and fellowship with each other. Without this bond, discipline is just punishment, conversation is just talking at each other, and a family is just another group of people. With that bond, however, everything changes. It compensates for mistakes, changes minds and hearts, and focuses the future of each family member on the target of living God's purpose for their lives. It is what makes a family a family for holidays and other gatherings for years to come.

NOTE

1.   Jack P. Shonkoff, et al., "The Science of Neglect: The Persistent Absence of Responsive Care Disrupts Brain Development," Center for the Developing Child at Harvard University, A Working Paper (2012), 2; www.developingchild.harvard.edu.

Chapter Nine

FROM LAW TO GRACE

God is kind, but he's not soft. In kindness he takes us firmly by the hand and leads us into a radical life-change. —ROMANS 2:4 MSG

As our children enter their pre-teen years, our goals and objectives change dramatically in how we raise them. In early childhood, the objective was to set protective limits, discipline to encourage correct behavior within those limits, and to convey the beginnings of a black-and-white sense of morality and justice. As they enter their early teen years, however, we build upon that foundation, but now begin to take the limits off to see if a sense of right and wrong has been internalized. We discipline more with consequences to help them understand what it means to be responsible for one's actions. We begin to teach more about the why behind what we believe. We help develop logical thinking, and we are willing to discuss issues with them as one adult to another rather than always as an adult to a child.

In childhood, we relied upon external controls and disciplined our children toward compliance; as they enter their teens, we must trust that God's laws have been written on their hearts and rely on their willingness to direct their lives by principles we hope they learned in childhood. Previously, we required only obedience; now we must move to the ministry of grace and understanding, teaching and response, relationship, and sound judgment. Even though they are not adults yet, by the time they hit thirteen, they have to learn to be governed by God's leading and their own sound decision making. Thank God we are still with them to help coach and counsel them through this next stage of life.

At the risk of being redundant, we want to acknowledge again that it is at this stage of development that many children are lost when parents fail to adapt to who their children are becoming. External rules and regulations will never be a substitute for the internal Golden Rule: *"In everything, therefore, treat people the same way you want them to treat you, for this is the Law and the Prophets"* (Matt. 7:12). While we don't treat our children as equals—we are still paying for everything, after all, and have had a few more years figuring out this game of life that they can learn from—modeling proper behavior and respect toward them is more important than ever. We need to model the proper use of authority and exemplify good leadership to them. Can we remain kind while disciplining them? Can we express our confidence and trust in them even while we express our disappointment? Can we stand beside them while they face the consequences of bad decisions? Or do we belittle and berate? Do we lecture and nag? Can we continue to express our love even in the midst of handing out consequences for their disrespect or rebellious actions or attitudes?

In his insightful book, *Parent Fuel,* author Barry St. Clair rightfully points out that many of us have put the ladder up against the wrong wall with our teens.[1] Parenting teens is so much more than just dealing with our children's behavior. For the first time in their lives, the teen years give our kids the opportunity to develop a vibrant walk with Jesus Christ. Out of that relationship comes the obedience and heart for doing right that guarantees success in life as they go out on their own.

If we fail to help them develop that heart, who will help them down the road, especially when most of our kids are abandoning church once they leave their parents' homes? We must help them move from the rules and regulations that made sense to them as children to the understanding of right, wrong, and grace that will make them a valuable and successful part of the adult world. They must learn the walk of love and go beyond the world of legalism.

There are difficulties in graduating from childhood to adulthood, however. For one, spending time with your children is more important than ever in their adolescent years, but more difficult to find. We need to transition our children from being governed solely by rules and regulations to being directed by grace, but the concept of grace is not an easy one to convey. Most Christian parents know little of the grace of God themselves and have never come to a place of walking in it, so we have some learning to do before we can teach it to our children. Few seem to really understand grace as it is expressed in the Bible. Too many turn instead to a long list of definitions and guidelines that try to describe what living by grace is, but fail to understand how to practice it. This then becomes just another form of legalism. Because of this, experiencing the victory of true Christian living is all too absent from the lives of most of God's people today.

For many believers, Christianity is a performance-based religion. Compliance to the "standards" of God is forced with the external controls of implied or threatened judgment, chastisement, punishment, and even rejection. In the bondage of repeated failure to walk in consistent victory over sin and selfishness, we live a life of repeated failure with the guilt and anxiety that can go along with that. This is exactly the religion that our children are choosing to leave behind as they go off to college, find full-time employment, and get married to start their own families. For them, there is no power or joy in living like that, because quite frankly, that is a powerless, legalistic take on Christianity.

God's real plan for our lives is very different, however. If there is one passage that describes how He really meant things to be, it is this one from the book of Galatians:

> *As long as the heir is a minor, he has no advantage over the slave. Though legally he owns the entire inheritance, he is subject to tutors and administrators until whatever date the father has set for emancipation. That is the way it is with us: When we were minors, we were just like slaves ordered around by simple instructions (the tutors and administrators of this world), with no say in the conduct of our own lives.*
>
> *But when the time arrived that was set by God the Father, God sent his Son, born among us of a woman, born under the conditions of the law so that he might redeem those of us who have been kidnapped by the law. Thus we have been set free to experience our rightful heritage. You can tell for sure that you are now fully adopted as his own children because God sent the Spirit of his Son into our lives crying out, "Papa! Father!" Doesn't that privilege of intimate conversation with God make it plain that you are not a slave, but a child? And if you are a child, you're also an heir, with complete access to the inheritance* (Galatians 4:1-7 MSG).

In one of Paul's other letters, he calls us "*heirs of God and fellow heirs with Christ*" (Rom. 8:17), meaning that, like children left a great estate, we have been given access to the kingdom of our Father in Heaven, just as Jesus has. We can call God "our Father" and speak directly to Him in prayer.

This passage makes a parallel between the walk of the people of God coming into a relationship with God and the walk of a prince coming into his inheritance as a king. The passage states that even though the prince actually owns the entire kingdom, while he is a child, he has no more rights than a slave. He is put under rules and regulations, teachers, guardians, and trainers, living under their authority and learning what is right and wrong until the age that his father, the present king, has determined he is old enough to think and manage himself according to principles he has internalized. Is he now a person of self-control, wisdom, and responsibility? The Law and overseers were there to teach him these things, but once he had a sense of it for himself, then he could have access to all that was left to him by his father, because now he can be trusted to do what is right with it.

The Bible teaches us that the Law is good because it has a specific function. It was designed to bring human beings to the realization of our total inadequacy to keep the Law of God and live a life that glorifies God without His help. But it is most important for us to see that, through the Law, God revealed that *righteousness cannot come from external rules and regulations.* The only way that the Law can produce anything that looks like righteousness is if we continue to live as slaves subject to the judgment and authority of others, but then even that eventually falls short. True righteousness only comes through Christ, His lordship, and the new laws of love and grace. We have to grow up from being children into mature adults who can understand grace and love and how to apply them in our everyday lives.

Many Christians legalistically spend their whole lives focused on the "rules and regulations" of God. They become obsessed with not doing or looking wrong. So they spend their time searching the Scriptures for the rules of God so that they can follow them, believing that if they can just do enough right things, spiritual growth is assured and blessing is inevitable. Unfortunately, the only thing inevitable is frustration and failure. Any approach to Christian living that relies on keeping rules as the path to spiritual growth, victory, and blessing is legalism. If we are living by legalism, we are not accepting the grace offered us by God. We are instead trying to earn our way to Heaven—an impossible task, because nothing but the grace of God can deliver us from our self-ish natures.

Rules have never delivered anyone from selfishness; they only bring people to the place of understanding their inability to do anything to remedy their own egocentric nature. Laws cannot make us *righteous*, which simply means "right with—having access to—God." As Paul wrote, "*By the works of the Law no flesh will be justified in His sight; for through the Law comes the knowledge of sin*" (Rom. 3:20). Think about that. The Law shouts, "You are no good; you are a failure; you can't do anything right; you are a sinner; you will never be what God wants; you must try harder; your performance is unacceptable; you are inadequate; you just won't do; in fact, no matter how hard you try, you won't be able to do it. Wake up and smell the coffee—the truth is you are worthless." Who can bear such reproach for long? Legalism can't help but say just the opposite of what love says. If we parent our children with Law instead of love and grace, this is the message they receive, and doubly so as we pass them from our jurisdiction to God's. Is it any wonder young adults are walking away from their faith in such large numbers today?

Yes, the Law is good; and yes, it has a place. Its place is to bring us to brokenness, to the understanding of our need for God's love and that grace is the only thing that can overcome our faults. But realizing our need for something is not the same as having it. The only way to be saved is if that thing we can't earn on our own is given to us by Someone worthy enough to earn it. Thus it is "*by grace you have been saved through faith; and that not of yourselves, it is the gift of God; not as a result of works*" (Eph. 2:8-9).

When we realize our brokenness and inadequacy, grace must be granted for growth to continue. If Law is continued when grace is required, the result is devastating. The Law then begins to arouse sin and rebellion, because legalism is not about relationship or the condition of our hearts, it is just about outward behavior. It cannot convey love. For the Christian, legalism means a life of struggle with sin and inconsistency that won't go away. For a child in training, it means a constant struggle to measure up only to find failure, frustration, and finally to abandon the faith in defeat and disillusionment. As Romans again describes it:

> For while we were in the flesh, the sinful passions, which were aroused by the Law, were at work in the members of our body to bear fruit for death. But now we have been released from the Law, having died to that by which we were bound, so that we serve in newness of the Spirit and not in oldness of the letter [of the law] (Romans 7:5-6).

Upon our salvation, God intended that we graduate from Law to grace.

> Therefore there is now no condemnation for those who are in Christ Jesus. For the law of the Spirit of life in Christ Jesus has set you free from the law of sin and of death. For what the Law could not do, weak as it was through the flesh, God did: sending His own Son in the likeness of sinful flesh and as an offering for sin, He condemned sin in the flesh, so that the requirement of the Law might be fulfilled in us, who do not walk according to the flesh but according to the Spirit (Romans 8:1-4).

God's concern with us is not about rules and regulations, but relationship to Him. When we became Christians, we did more than just change the rules we live by. We entered into a relationship with the living God through His living Son, Jesus Christ. We have become the adopted heirs of God! This is why Paul chastises in Galatians 4:6-7 (MSG):

> You can tell for sure that you are now fully adopted as his own children because God sent the Spirit of his Son into our lives

crying out, "Papa! Father!" Doesn't that privilege of intimate conversation with God make it plain that you are not a slave, but a child? And if you are a child, you're also an heir, with complete access to the inheritance.

No longer are we governed by external controls or rules to have access to God, we have but to call out His name in prayer and we can have *"intimate conversation"* with our Papa! (Or as we would say today, our "Dad.") He has also given us a new heart with "internal controls" written right into its DNA. No longer are we to be changed by the external, but now we are changed by the internal desire of our hearts as we comprehend through the revelation and illumination of the Holy Spirit what God has already done and provided for us. We are transformed by the very nature of Jesus as we walk with Him in intimacy, communion, and deep fellowship. He is literally the fulfillment of all the rules and regulations as His life flows into ours. We exude His grace and love as we absorb it from Him.

GRACEFUL PARENTING

So, as we approach the task of parenting our teens, it is vitally important that we understand that we can never make enough rules to protect them from every evil to which they will be exposed—and if we could, such a structure of regulations would be smothering! Instead, we must lead them to a place where they may develop a sincere heart for the living God on their own. The center of our instruction must be Jesus Christ Himself and not some system of performance meant to somehow satisfy the societal norms of our Christian communities. We spend most of our time trying to develop teens who will do right and not do wrong when, in fact, we should be spending our time teaching them how to better seek Jesus and apprehend His life. This is so important that the apostle Paul readily denounced all his past accomplishments, including the finest education available in his day, his reputation for sacrifice and zeal above his peers, and many awards and accomplishments within the Jewish faith in favor of a knowledge of God that would lead him to righteousness in Christ.

> *But whatever things were gain to me, those things I have counted as loss for the sake of Christ. More than that, I count all things to be loss in view of the surpassing value of knowing Christ Jesus my Lord, for whom I have suffered the loss of all things, and count them but rubbish so that I may gain Christ, and may be found in Him, not having a righteousness of my own derived from the Law, but that which is through faith in Christ, the righteousness which comes from God on the basis of faith* (Philippians 3:7-9).

What does this mean to us as parents? It means that we must do more than just establish standards and police them. We must work with our growing children to teach them the biblical reasons behind principles and boundaries. Exposure to the heart of God produces a hunger and thirst to know and please Him. It doesn't mean that there are no limits. God places restrictions upon us all, for both guidance and protection, just as any parent would. It means instead that we must take the time to teach them the Word of God and nature of Christ so that our teens will understand the necessity for boundaries and willingly submit to them out of a heart for God. More so, when they learn to pull satisfaction out of life through knowing Christ, the false promises of temptations lose their appeal. When they understand this, teens often set better boundaries for themselves than we would have chosen for them as parents. It is an incredible experience when our children start to set examples we are challenged to live up to!

Most of us were brought up under the merit system of acceptance and reward. That is fine for the world, but it does not empower us to live in the Kingdom of God. In reality, we have spent most of our lives trying to live up to someone's expectations in order to gain their approval—first our parents, then our friends, then perhaps an employer, and eventually maybe even a spouse. And when all that's done, there's always someone willing to point out how much we have fallen short.

However, grace says, "I love and accept you not based upon what you do, but rather who you are and who you are becoming. You are my child and I love you, unconditionally, not based upon your character, but based solely upon the character I—God—have placed in you. There is nothing you have done or could do that would cause Me to reject you as My child. My love is always available to you. I will never leave you nor forsake you."

Philippians 2:13 takes it further telling us: *"For it is God who is at work in you, both to will and to work for His good pleasure."* Grace is not only unconditional love and acceptance, it is God's desire and His power working in us to accomplish His will in our lives and the lives of those we touch. So, grace further says, "You can do this because I will help you. My power is sufficient, rest in Me. I will teach you. I will instruct you. I will show you how. Failure is never final. You are capable of overcoming—all things are possible to them who trust in Me for I will be their strength." This is the role of the grace-filled parent as well. We are an instructor, a leader, an encourager, an exhorter, and a comforter. We are a cheerleader for and reminder of what God is doing in our children's lives as they grow into His destiny for them.

As they grow up and near adulthood, our role is not to administer punishment for broken standards or foolish mistakes. God is not punitive. The natural consequences of our mistakes or bad decisions are punishment enough for us, why shouldn't the same work for our teens? Our role is to administer justice and allow the cause-and-effect sequences and the reproofs of life to teach the final lessons, not punishments that we contrive. Basically that amounts to holding our kids accountable to "fix" whatever they have "broken," or to make right with whomever they have wronged. We can then stand with them in counseling how to do those things, while at the same time holding them accountable to do what is right.

For example, what if a curfew is broken? Justice would possibly be restriction from a particular activity for a specific amount of time proportionate to the broken standard, or loss of the use of the family car because of their broken word—both are natural consequences of violated trust. We once heard of a set of parents who restricted their teen for three years for one broken curfew! That's not grace; that's a prison sentence! Not to mention the three-year loss of teaching opportunities while the child was restricted. How is a teen supposed to learn from mistakes they are never allowed to make?

Grace allows decisions to be made by our teens—even when they don't necessarily choose as we would—so that they learn from correct *and* incorrect choices. If they aren't allowed to make them under our supervision, how will we guide their learning from them? Just be sure that the risk involved with a wrong or poor decision is equal to the level of maturity shown.

Demonstrated responsibility must yield increased freedom just as surely as demonstrated irresponsibility yields a loss of freedom and increased supervision. This is where the rubber meets the road. Too often parents restrict freedom when teens act irresponsibly, but they are reluctant to grant increased freedom and privilege when responsibility is shown. Obsessive and neurotic parents are bad about this. We tend to remember how foolish we were at their age and we fear our kids will make the same mistakes we did. But then we forget that is exactly the idea! While some reserve may be warranted, if we have done our job as parents, we need to realize our teens have a greater heart for God than we did and will probably make better choices. Chances are that our kids will be better prepared to deal with the dangers that go with the increased freedom if they've learned those lessons earlier in life, when the costs were low—rather than later when they are higher.

THE BOTTOM LINE

If our children are to succeed in life, they must go from living by an exterior set of rules and regulations to being driven by an internal sense of purpose, a positive outlook on life, and an ethical backbone of doing good and not harm. Though this begins with a form of "law" regarding how to live when they are younger, it becomes a "way" of grace when they are older. They become able to determine what is the right thing to do in each new circumstance of life, not based on memorized rules, but with a balance of the cognitive analysis of the brain and the compassionate mandates of the heart. This doesn't come overnight, but is developed over time through learning to make good—and bad!—decisions (we do often learn more from our mistakes, after all), as they seek to live by an inner light rather than the demands and standards of those around them.

Grace looks into the life of our children and sees the masterpiece they are before God. Then grace acts to draw forth the genius of who they really are. As we do that with our children, we teach them to do the same with others. This is the process that not only turns our children into adults, but puts them far ahead of the game toward being all God has called them to be.

NOTE

1.   Barry St. Clair, *Parent Fuel* (Wheaton, IL: Crossway Books, 2007).

Chapter Ten

ENJOYING ADOLESCENCE

Although my parents had clear boundaries for us, they had few
rules. Their boundaries were walls that did not move, but we
had freedom within them. I had no curfew, and I was given
the responsibility to make my own moral choices. I was also
burdened with the consequences; I knew that, although they
would still love me, they would not rescue me from my wrong
choices. —MONTE SWAN, *Romancing Your Child's Heart*[1]

A young father attended a parenting seminar put on by a fellow minister and friend of ours. During a question and answer session, he voiced some serious concerns. He started by describing a near-perfect son from infancy through his early teen years. But then, suddenly, seemingly out of nowhere, it was as if someone had put a giant syringe in the young man's ear and sucked out all of his brains. His grades dropped. He began arguing incessantly with his parents. His attitude became very negative about almost everything, and it appeared the direction of his life had changed dramatically for the worse. The perplexed father ended his description by saying, "All this child training stuff looks good on paper, but it doesn't really work. My boy grew up in a Christian home, was in church every time the doors were opened, and was educated in the finest Christian school in our area. But look at him now!"

What had happened? Why did things change so severely when this son hit adolescence?

Well, speaking a little further with this father, it turned out that he had left the training of his child mainly to his church and the Christian school, neglecting to set and enforce proper boundaries at home. This led to the parents being able to "corral" their child while he was smaller, but when he hit his teens and puberty, the changes that go along with this new stage of life threw everything up into the air. Because a baseline of respect and relationship had not been established when their son was younger, everything backfired as their son began the questioning and striving for self-definition that is the normal territory of adolescence. It appeared that these parents, despite their best intents, had mistaken "exposure" for training.

Training, by definition, requires that the person be conditioned and equipped to be able to perform certain skills proficiently. Simply exposing a child to a Christian home and sending him or her to a church or Christian school is not training. Remember that being part of a good environment does not guarantee "good" children. They have to be trained, disciplined, and educated in right and wrong. Education, in fact, is much more than just academics. Teaching must embrace the very heart and character of a child, not just fill his or her head with knowledge. The finest Christian surroundings and schooling will be ineffective if the child has not been trained to respect and obey authority by the two most influential adults in every child's life—*the child's parents*.

J. Richard Fugate, director of the Foundation for Biblical Research and author of *What the Bible Says about Child Training*, writes this concerning the role of parents:

> If you desire for your child to become obedient and willing
> to accept God's standards as his [or her] own, you will have

to utilize the process that God has designed to obtain these results. Biblical child training produces a quality character much different than would have naturally developed had the child been left alone to grow up according to his [or her] own nature.[2]

Our role as parents is to be a tool in the hands of God used to train our children in character, respect for others, and purpose. This involves restraining our children's natural tendencies toward selfishness and rebellion against authority from the time they are young. It also involves teaching, discipling, and mentoring them within defined limits and enforced boundaries. As parents, we discipline our children to help them understand these restrictions and to think more about their actions and decisions than we as parents do. Then as they grow and mature, we nudge them toward a sense of morality that is not ruled by legalistic rules and regulations, but recognizes right and wrong based on the grace and love of God. They begin to recognize the benefits and joys of a life ruled by the principle of treating others just as they would like to be treated themselves—according to the Golden Rule.

To put it bluntly, neither the church nor the schools can resurrect what the home has put to death. If children don't learn these things from their parents, chances are they will never learn them anywhere else. (Thank God, of course, that there are exceptions to that rule, but the more sure thing is that we train our children ourselves!)

FACING "THE BIG CHANGE"

Now, in all of this, we don't want to minimize what happens when our children hit puberty and adolescence. In addition to the hormonal changes and mood swings, kids go through a full brain rewiring. Even the most well disciplined of children with strong bonds of love with their parents will act out to challenge their elders, question what you believe and stand for, and pull stunts that are stupider than anything they might have tried as children. Not only that, but they have more dangerous things to do it with. They are now driving, are out more often and later than they were as children, and are reaching their peak of physical strength while their brains are caught between the highest level of intellectual thought and being doused with hormones they have never experienced before.

Now, hear us in this, though many secular psychologists call these things normal—stating, "Rebellion is just a part of adolescence as your young adults begin to seek more independence and begin to define what they believe and what they don't for themselves"—we do not believe that "normal" is the same thing as "acceptable," as many seem to interpret it. Certainly, rebellion is a normal part of adolescence—as it is a part of childhood, though to a lesser degree—but that only means that we should expect it, not that we should allow it! Any of us, without having the proper training from childhood or the love and grace of God in our lives to point us to a better way, would "naturally" be selfish and rebellious. Even with such advantages, we still fight to overcome these vices and only succeed because we embrace the work God is doing in our lives. We need to be authoritative—not authoritarian—guides to our adolescents so they can make the same transition from being under the rules of guardians as children to being adults who can make their own decisions according to grace and a loving respect for others.

Adolescence is a confusing time for both parents and teens. By now, a great deal of work has been done to form your teen's personality and hopefully by this time your children are young believers in Christ anxious to find their place in the Kingdom of God. However, be that as it may, this is still a time of great transition. As with any big change, there is also a great deal of confusion due to transforming roles, responsibilities, and physical abilities. Many times new expectations and duties require wisdom, knowledge, skills, and understanding your children have yet to possess. At times they are treated like adults and at other times like children. When to allow your teens to make their own decisions and when you should hold on to the decision-making power yourself can be the center of a great many controversies. It's very unlikely you will get it right every time.

The goal of your teaching by this time in their lives is to help your teens move from external controls to internal controls, from dependence upon you to dependence upon God and an internalized sense of right and wrong. We are moving from rules and regulations to grace, from forced compliance to willing submission to proper authority. Therefore, teaching at this stage is much more than simply establishing limitations and demanding compliance. We are exposing our children to the three characteristics of maturity:

1. *Knowledge*—the ability to see things from God's point of view.

2. *Wisdom*—the ability to respond to life situations with Christlike character.

3. *Understanding*—the ability to capture the heart of God and the very thoughts behind His actions.

We need to go into this time of life with our eyes wide open. A middle school teacher friend of ours calls seventh grade (when most kids reach the age of thirteen) the *"sproing"* year. It's as if there's a big spring that is released within them—*"Sproing!"*—and every principle, belief, and conviction that wasn't firmly "nailed down" in childhood goes flying in every direction. He noted that sixth graders start to show some signs of this by the end of the year, seventh grade classes can be incredibly unpredictable (he affectionately calls them "Nerf balls" as they tend to bounce off the walls, but don't really hurt anything), and then they begin to settle down a bit by the end of eighth grade. This is certainly a time of great change!

We need to note, as well, that adolescence is really a product of the twentieth century, created by the industrial age and the requirement for teenagers to attend secondary school rather than staying home to work with their parents on the family farm or homestead. George Washington, for example, was the official surveyor for Culpepper County, Virginia at the age of seventeen. David Farragut, the first admiral of the United State Navy and a hero during the Civil War, took command of his first ship at the age of twelve. Clara Barton, the founder of the Red Cross, nursed her brother back to health when she was only twelve and then at fourteen took on the responsibility for what grew into a ward of smallpox patients during an outbreak in her hometown. Up through the end of the nineteenth century, there was only childhood and then adulthood. Coming of age ceremonies like Bar Mitzvahs ushered thirteen-year-olds from childhood into young adulthood. They were boys and girls, and then young men and women—no stage in between. In fact, the first time the term *teenager* appeared in the dictionary was in 1961! Today, in the first decades of the twenty-first century, where adolescence used to be the property of the teenage years, the attitude and lack of adult behavior no longer ends when a young person hits twenty or even the magical age of twenty-one. Now, adolescence seems to last—for some—all the way into their early thirties!

What is the reason for this? We are sure there are several, but one of the main ones has to be the lowering of expectations we have for our young people from roughly thirteen through when they graduate from college and often even into their early career years. As never before, our kids are coddled and allowed to laze around the house watching TV or playing video games. Rarely are they responsible for any chores or contributing to the household in any meaningful way. Then, after college, how often do they show up at their parents' front door looking for a place to live "until they can get themselves a little more settled"?

Now, our purpose here is not to rant about our changing times. Cultures change every few years and provide us, as parents, new challenges. For the most part, however, these are surface issues. Character is still character, right is still right, and wrong is still wrong. The Golden Rule and "love your neighbor as yourself" are still the best guideposts for morality. The problem isn't that society has changed—though we have to admit we don't agree with many of the changes around us, and they certainly don't seem to be making things easier for most people—but that our expectations of what our kids are capable of have changed. We have gotten caught up in the flow of cultural opinions, and as happens when you go with the flow, just like with a river, your path tends to be crooked and downhill.

So instead of setting solid boundaries for our kids and raising expectations age-appropriately as they grow, we tend to instead placate, manipulate, badger, and coddle from the time they hit middle school until they graduate from college—and our kids are the worse for it. We often think it is not that big a deal and we make excuses, but take a look at this list from the Houston Police Department that was published back in the 1960s—their "Twelve Rules for Raising Delinquent Children":

1. Begin with infancy to give your children everything they want. In this way, they will grow up to believe the world owes them a living.

2. When children pick up bad words and mannerisms, laugh at them. This will make them think they are "cute." It will also encourage them to pick up "cuter" phrases down the road and adopt conduct that will stagger you later.

3. Never give them any spiritual training or require accountability to God. Wait till your children are twenty-one, and then let them make their own decisions about what to believe without you prejudicing them.

4. Avoid use of the word "wrong" and avoid shame and conviction at all costs. It may develop a guilt complex. Don't limit their creativity by restricting their actions. This will condition them to believe later, when they are arrested for

stealing a car, for example, that society is against them and they are being persecuted.

5. Pick up everything they leave lying around—books, shoes, and clothing. Avoid holding them accountable for their own problems and do everything for them so they will be experienced in throwing all responsibility onto others.

6. Let them read any printed matter and listen to anything they can get their hands on or that their "friends" give them. Let them watch whatever they want on TV. Don't invade their privacy by concerning yourself with what is in their diary, what they look at, or what they listen to. Be careful that the silverware and drinking glasses are sterilized, but let their mind feast on whatever they want.

7. Quarrel with your spouse frequently in the presence of your children. In this way, they will not be too shocked when the home is broken up later.

8. Give children all the spending money they want. Never encourage them to earn their own money to buy what they want. Why should they have things as tough as you had them?

9. Satisfy your children's every craving for food, drink, and comfort. See that every sensual desire is gratified. Denial may lead to harmful frustration.

10. Always take your children's side against neighbors, teachers, police officers, coaches, and other authority figures. They are all prejudiced against your children anyway—how could it be your kids who are actually at fault?

11. When your children get into real trouble, apologize for yourself by saying, "I never could do anything with that

kid." Absolve yourself of responsibility by saying, "Why is my child like this? I didn't raise him (or her) that way!"

12.   Allow your children to choose their own friends and never criticize them even for the worst of transgressions. This will only lead to low self-esteem. Be your children's friend and not a control freak so that they will "love" you and not resent you for acting like a parent, even if they never show you any respect.

If you properly do all of these, then prepare for a life of grief. You are apt to have one![3]

If these things were that obvious fifty years ago, do we really think they will get us any better results today when cultural expectations are so much more lax? No wonder we have teen crime and drug and alcohol abuse at unprecedented levels!

SOLID BOUNDARIES SET OUR CHILDREN FREE

Boundaries give children a sense of security and establish an environment in which it is safe to explore and learn. If you have a front yard and there is no fence between your yard and the street, you warn your children about the dangers of the street. You tell them to avoid strangers. You tell them what can happen when a car comes by. You tell them to be very, very careful and to stay in the yard. And what happens? Your children can go out and play in the front yard, but they stay right next to the house, far away from the street, because they know there is danger there. If you want to increase the play area for your children, you know what you can do? You put up a fence; you erect a protective boundary between the yard and the street. When you put that up, it increases their play area. Now they can run right up to that fence—they will run all around that yard—and know they are perfectly safe as long as they don't go outside of it. You have increased their freedom because of the solid boundary.

Boundaries and limits prepare our kids for societal living from infancy through graduation from high school. Some children don't believe the rules apply to them. Make sure your boundaries are clear. The reason kids skirt around boundaries is—as noted in the list from the Houston Police Department—that parents never put solid, clear restrictions on these children when they were younger, so they are inexperienced with learning to internalize these limits when they are older. Simply put, they have never developed self-control, because they never had fences to test their ability to control their behaviors.

Boundaries teach our children about the consequences of disregard. They must learn early that the choices they make determine the path they take and ultimately the future they create. All standards must be clearly established. Disciplining your child—especially a preteen or teen—for standards not clearly stated can stimulate rebellion and close your child's heart to further instruction. Keep things simple, especially with verbal instructions. Multiple commands at once can be confusing. Because of brain changes, teens may actually have difficulty assimilating multiple-stepped instructions. Therefore, it is imperative that the standard be clearly communicated even to the point of having them repeat your instructions back to you.

The best standards are those you have established with your teen through your instruction and leadership. When dealing with detailed standards like those for dating, it is good to actually put them in writing. This works well for chores and household policies, too. If you are unable to agree upon the established standards, of course, your decision as parents is final, but always remember that your goal is to move your teen toward internal controls—the rules kids keep the best are the ones they help set. You want to teach your children to make the right decision on their own. So let your teens help make decisions whenever possible.

The boundaries you set represent your value system as a parent. Don't make standards that are inconsistent with who you are or who you aspire to be. Don't try to enforce strong boundaries for your children when you have absolutely none for yourself. You can make boundaries that challenge yourself to grow, though, and set the right example for your kids as you meet and exceed your own goals.

Once you put them in place, you must stand by them, or they do little good. In fact, you should look forward to opportunities to enforce them. That's right. Not only should you expect them to be broken, but look forward to it! As mentioned previously, every opportunity you have to enforce a low-costing boundary or standard is mileage toward keeping your kids from making the high-costing ones down the road.

As godly parents, we must learn to appreciate those times of instruction that come with confrontation, conflict, and resolution after a boundary has been broken. Without them, no changes occur in the wills of our children. Your clashes with the will of your child will not last forever. When dealt with properly and consistently, a child's will is usually brought into submission rather quickly. Start early when your child is most pliable, and the job will be easier than if you start late. Once you go head to head and establish your parental right to rule, however, things get a lot better and you'll be tested only occasionally just to be sure the fences are still in place. However, to do this properly you must be able to determine when to bear down and when to lighten up. Like God the Father, there are times to discipline in grace and times to offer mercy.

In his book *Secrets of the Vine*, Bruce Wilkerson outlines God's approach to chastisement as being three steps.[4] First comes verbal rebuke, followed by temporal consequences, and finally in the presence of a lack of repentance, chastening. For the adult, these can come over time or in rapid succession. We are rebuked by God through the Word, a message preached, the admonition of a friend, or the simple, direct conviction of the Holy Spirit. Failure to respond and repent leads to the natural consequences of the sin coming to bear fully upon us. This may range from physical or material losses to relational problems with those we love. Until we learn our lesson and come to God for His help, He will keep working on us to help us grow. His boundaries and lessons for us are never arbitrary. He is always working to bring us closer to Him and make us more fruitful in relating to others.

THE BOTTOM LINE

Why do we have boundaries? The purpose of boundaries is to protect from dangers, to restrain evil, and to regulate good. That is the purpose of our legal system, and these things work the same way in our homes. Children are born without internal controls—those controls that fence out dangers and moderate correct behavior. Laws and rules keep the child protected while they are in the process of forming those internal controls better known as good judgment, morality, and wisdom. Boundaries also give children a territory within which to explore freely without fear. What happens when they cross such boundaries in acts of disobedience or rebellion? We are presented with a teaching moment that can speed up the learning of those internal controls!

Solid boundaries provide our children with security and significance. Solid boundaries give them feelings of stability and well-being in spite of the circumstances around them, and provide meaning and purpose in life as they form their own moral compasses. Setting such limits erects walls of protection in order to set our children free. This will also help them to have a positive influence on the lives of others as they mature. When they are clear and properly enforced, we give our children freedom to learn and make low-cost mistakes that will teach them decision-making skills. This will save them from stress and heartache later in life. They also allow our interactions with our children to be focused on a common set of shared values and make our home a more pleasant place to be.

NOTES

1. Monte Swan, *Romancing Your Child's Heart* (Sisters, OR: Loyal Publishing, 2002), 86.

2. J. Richard Fugate, *What the Bible Says about Child Training* (Foundation for Biblical Research, 1980, 1996), 84.

3. "Twelve Rules for Raising Delinquent Children" drawn up by the police department of Houston, Texas; as quoted in Larry Christenson, *The Christian Family* (1970), 88 (edited and updated).

4. Bruce Wilkinson, *Secrets of the Vine* (Sisters, OR: Multnomah Publishers, 2001), 45-50.

Chapter Eleven

EDIFYING WORDS EMPOWER

*The future of America will not be determined by presidents
or politicians, but instead by what parents teach or fail
to teach their children. Therefore, bless your children
in the name of the Lord. Release the power of God into
their lives with spoken blessings.* —JOHN HAGEE

The art of discipling our children in this way is twofold. We are to raise them in the nurture and admonition of the Lord. This means correction by chastisement, and also correction by encouragement. However, we tend to be long on chastisement and short on encouragement.

Too many of us want our children to be well balanced, well groomed, and well manicured, not for the sake of the children, but so that we can look good in the eyes of others. We correct the easier exterior issues without occupying ourselves with the issues of the heart. Constant correction alone does not raise our children up in the way they should go. We must make investments into our children's spirits and souls, and this comes through speaking words of life and blessing over them, continually.

It is important to understand what are words of life and what aren't. Empty praise is not full of life. There was a trend in the 1970s in education to give children constant positive feedback, no matter what they did or how they did it. The thought was that this "unconditional positive regard" would seep into the children's self-concepts and eventually they would perform better as they felt better about themselves. What we ended up with instead was a generation of kids who felt really good about who they were *as they did wrong*—whether that meant wrong answers or wrong behavior. Other children it just drove more deeply into poor self-image, because they recognized the praise was hollow and insincere, and that, in the end, there was no love in it.

A biblical self-image is one thing, while the world's idea of self-love simply magnifies problems already beginning in the hearts of our children. Pastor, Bible teacher, and author John MacArthur writes:

> The truth is that much of the modern effort to spark kid's self-esteem is simply pouring gasoline on a runaway fire. It encourages already selfish kids to think they are justified in wanting their own way. It makes parents think they must defer to the child, no matter what, because the child has a right to express himself freely, so that he feels good about himself. All this only escalates out-of-control behavior and feeds all the worst tendencies of human depravity.[1]

When we allow society to determine who we are, we take the first steps toward diminishing the potential God has placed in us. We will wind up at the airport when our ship comes in every time. We dare not allow who we are, our value as an individual, or our place in society to be determined by anyone but our heavenly Father. He is the only one who truly has knowledge of these things, for He is the one who created us according to His divine will and purpose for our lives. The world tells us that it's our parents, our possessions, and our position in society that determine who we are. My value as a person—according to society—is determined by my physical appearance, my talents and abilities, and my performance, whether it is poor, average, or superior. Whether a person's life is seen as significant or not is totally based on the approval of others, the recognition, and the reward they receive for all they have achieved on the outside during their lives.

On the other end of the spectrum, I was recently told the story of a successful young go-getter whose colleagues noticed that she left promptly at 4:00 p.m. every Friday afternoon, even though the workday didn't end until 5:00. It was especially significant because everything else she did so exuded excellence that others noticed her; ducking out early every Friday afternoon seemed out of character, to say the least.

In the course of events, one of her fellow employees asked her where she went every Friday afternoon. "I go to my parents for Shabbat service. I have to leave early because they live two hours away."

"Oh, so it is because of your religion?" he commented.

Sheepishly, she looked down at the floor, and then answered, "Not completely. You see, every Friday evening, as part of the ceremony, my father speaks a blessing over each of us children. It's hard to explain, but I can't miss that blessing. It means too much. It has been such an important part of my life that it is worth the two hours there and the two hours back each weekend so that my father can speak his blessings over me."

Truthfully, we have no real idea of the impact of our words on our children. What we speak to them matters—they hear it, they digest it, and that little mastermind in their subconscious internalizes those words to construct the child's self-image. Depending on what we speak, either that little mastermind loses its diabolical nature or it worsens. Constant negatives clog up the energy pathways of our children's souls like plaque in an artery. Our words can cut off the life flow meant to come out of our children and touch the world, or they can release and increase it.

Social science research tells us that by the time a child is five years old, that child has heard the word "No," on average, 40,000 times and the word "Yes" only 8,000 times. That's a five to one ratio! That's a little lopsided toward the negative, don't you think? Now we know that "No" is a necessary word for children growing up—"No, you may not stick your finger in that electrical socket." "No, don't eat that partially opened candy bar you found on the street!" "No, you may not bring home that skunk as a pet." "Don't hit your sister!" "Don't touch that!" "Don't wander off at the mall!" "Don't! Don't! Don't! No! No! *No!*" We never thought about this constant barrage of negatives with our own kids until we read this statistic and paid attention to this constant flow of "No"s with our grandchildren. We started wondering if it wasn't important to balance out all of these "No"s with some positives about what they could do and that affirmed who they are.

As a whole, our society is big on correcting mistakes and not so great about recognizing and encouraging strengths. We think, "Well, you have such and such going for you—no need to mention any of that. Instead, let's see if we can't go over here and deal with these little toothpick problems to make you a better, more well-rounded person." But the truth of the matter is a person who just goes around trying to compensate for their weaknesses is seldom very successful. A person with a great personality doesn't take endless math classes to make up for a deficiency in that area. Instead, that person goes into sales or becomes a spokesperson promoting a cause or a company. He or she leaves the number crunching to someone who is good at that, but who may not like public speaking. We all have our strengths, and we tend to live by them more than we do by correcting our weaknesses.

In a negative world, if the positive is not given, the negative will be automatically assumed. Far too many kids in our nation are branded with labels that act as judgments on their characters. "He's so mean."

"She's so dumb." "I can't believe how clumsy you are!" "You lazy, good-for-nothing..." "Why can't you get grades like your sister? Are you the dumb one in the family or something?"

When children hear Mom or Dad say things about them, they endeavor to live up to what is said. When teachers, preachers, aunts, uncles, and the adults they admire say things about them, kids are impacted more than we realize. If we are trying to pull the best out of our children, shouldn't we pay attention to what we speak about them? Children need encouragement, praise, and positive reinforcement to overcome all of the negative that comes their way.

Proverbs says, *"Rash language cuts and maims, but there is healing in the words of the wise"* (Prov. 12:18 MSG). Kind words heal and help; cutting words wound and maim. Patience and persistence pierces through indifference. Gentle speech breaks down rigid defenses. *"Watch your words and hold your tongue; you'll save yourself a lot of grief"* (Prov. 21:23 MSG).

Make a point to correct your children without ever belittling them with your words, actions, or attitude. Training and correction are more for positive reinforcement for what is right than about what is wrong. Psychologists tell us that punishment can inhibit a particular behavior, but it does not guarantee that behavior will be replaced by something better, just by something new. Encouragement, however, reinforces good behaviors, and the more good behaviors we have, the less time we have to do wrong.

The value of a parent's encouragement appears to be especially important for fathers. Studies from penitentiaries show that virtually all inmates had bad relationships with their fathers, and when asked for reasons why, four out of the top five categories given had to do with the words the fathers spoke over their kids (the other was about the time they spent with them and the quality of their conversations together). Convicts reported that their fathers were:

1. always critical,

2. never admitted doing anything wrong or ever apologized for their actions,

3. rarely had time to really listen to them,

4. compared them regularly with other children, and

5. insensitive—using degrading terms like stupid, loser, no good, sissy, "you will never amount to anything," and phrases like that.

On the other hand, it is amazing how much children want to please their parents and be affirmed by them. When you say something like, "He's a great reader," then you will likely have a hard time catching your son without a book in the next few days. If you say, "She's a great runner!" Then your daughter is likely to look for excuses to run by you as often and as fast as she can!

THE POWER—AND AUTHORITY—TO BLESS

Previous generations did what is seldom, if ever, done today—speak daily blessings over the family and home. It was done regularly and on commemorative occasions. Speaking blessings used to be part of both Hebrew and Christian cultures. Though we don't seem to recognize the significance, speaking a "benediction" over a congregation at the end of a Sunday service is speaking a blessing to carry with them throughout the week. We have let this become such an empty ritual that many churches have done away with it.

Webster's Dictionary tells us that *to bless* means, "to invoke divine favor on, to bestow happiness, prosperity, or good things of all kinds; to make a pronouncement holy; to consecrate, to glorify for the benefits received, to extol for excellencies." Webster then defines a *blessing* as, "a prayer or solemn wish imploring happiness upon another; …that which promotes prosperity and welfare." In other words, *to bless* means to speak good rather than evil, to encourage rather than discourage, to project success rather than failure, to instill faith rather than doubt, to encourage boldness rather than fear, to impart hope rather than distress, and to share love rather than neglect.

If you think about it, you will realize that words are little packages of meaning that go straight to the heart—and our children hang on our every word, unless we have done something to close their hearts to us. Those little packages have the ability to inspire confidence, strengthen, convey wisdom, pique curiosity, give permission to explore, realize potential, and bring healing; or they can discourage, belittle, goad, destroy potential, limit, frustrate, and wound. We see in the Scriptures that God taught the Jews to bless or approve their children based on the fact that they belonged to God, not on their merit or worth. This was to be a lifestyle for them and was to happen daily, weekly, and monthly, as well as on special holidays or occasions. Jewish families still celebrate Bar Mitzvahs today—a special ceremony to inaugurate a young teen into adulthood by blessing them verbally and financially, giving them a foundational storehouse in the spirit and in the natural upon which to build their futures. Is it any wonder then that less than one percent of those incarcerated in our prisons today are of Jewish heritage? Such events and blessings carry great significance and power to propel our children toward good and not evil.

Such times of speaking a formal blessing usually have these five elements:

1. An encouraging and loving touch,

2. Meaningful spoken words,

3. High value attributed to the one being blessed,

4. A picture painted of a special future for the one being blessed, and

5. An active commitment to participate in the fulfilling of the blessing.

In his book *The Power of Spoken Blessing*, Bill Gothard included a letter from a couple in New Zealand about how speaking blessings transformed their sad, seven-year-old son and through him, their entire family:

> My husband and I noticed that our seven-year-old son, Samuel, was becoming characterized by a very miserable countenance, drooping shoulders, lips that go down instead of up, etc. Every attempt we made to correct the problem failed. We had reached a point of exasperation!
>
> It was around this time that we listened to two audiotapes by Bill Ligon, titled *How to Impart Blessings* and *Redemptive Power of the Blessing*. We also watched a video on the power of the spoken word and read the book, *The Power of Spoken Blessings*.... Through these materials, the Lord opened up our understanding of the power of the spoken word either as a blessing or as a curse.
>
> I remember the exciting revelation the Lord gave: "Samuel needs a blessing!"
>
> I gathered the other children around and blessed Samuel. I asked God to bless him with a radiant countenance, joy in his heart, and a beautiful smile that ministered to the lives of others.
>
> As I was speaking, his little face lit up, his chest puffed out, and he just kept smiling! I spoke the same blessing to him once more that week.
>
> It has been around six months now, and I am happy to report that the change in Samuel has been miraculous! He keeps smiling, has a radiant joy about him, and the first thing we notice about Samuel in the morning is a beautiful, radiant smile and a very enthusiastic "Good morning!" This has truly been a work

of the Lord, for all of our own efforts failed. In simple faith, we have been obedient and have witnessed the power of the spoken blessing!

We have noticed several things happen in our family as we apply the lessons learned in giving a blessing. We are all demonstrating more love toward each other. Our attitudes really are transformed by speaking blessings, and the children are growing in faith!

Our children will come to us and report that one of their siblings needs a blessing because he/she has a bad attitude, or we should bless this child because he/she is being naughty!

All of us then gather around and bless the "offender." This act demonstrates great love toward him/her. No need for telling tales or taking matters into their own hands, as they now have a practical solution to the situation!

Whenever my husband and I notice a wrong attitude in a child, that child receives a blessing, and I am continually amazed at how attitudes are changed immediately! Sometimes a little talk is required, but the spoken blessing is a transformer.[2]

Craig Hill, the director of Family Foundations International, makes this observation about the tragic results of parents in general, and fathers in particular, who do not speak blessings over their children:

Today, there is a lack of fathering and a lack of blessing and impartation, so people go in search of that blessing and of that manhood in all sorts of other ways. Some people go and join gangs—searching to become a man or a woman. Gangs, of course, have rites and mechanisms and ways that you can be accepted as a man or as a woman, by which you become a full-fledged member of that "family," so to speak. That happens when a blessing doesn't legitimately take place through a father.

Other people go in search of love and impartation through sexual promiscuity. Some people are drawn into homosexuality—young men in search of love and impartation that really should have come from a father. Others are drawn into sexual promiscuity with the opposite gender. Many types of things take place that are destructive maladies in our society today that pass from one generation to the next when blessings have not been imparted. And where there has been impartation and blessing and the release of identity and destiny to children, you see just the opposite result. These things will flow from one generation to the next. In other words, we tend to do to our children and treat our children in similar ways to how we were treated by our parents.[3]

Consider the power of the parental blessing. As a parent, you have the power to speak life or death into your children. Parent, when you call your son or daughter "stupid," "idiot," or "dumbbell," you have placed a curse upon their ability and motivation to learn! Instead, speak meaningful words of life over and into them—blessings, not cursings; ability, not shortcomings.

ROUTINES OF BLESSING

We truly believe that one of the most overlooked opportunities to bless not only our children, but also our families, is to eat meals together as regularly as possible. (We know we mentioned this before, but it bears repeating.) Such gatherings give our children the opportunity to be seen and heard in a setting like few others. Here, though the parents "chair" the meals, each person can be given the floor to tell about their day, talk about an issue, or give an opinion without anyone else interrupting. It gives you the opportunity to teach children the skills of polite conversation, the etiquette of friendly and sometimes not-so-friendly debate, as well as opportunities to learn how to express what they believe and why.

There are also resources such as Robert Crosby's book *Now We Are Talking* that give you age-appropriate discussion starters you might not think of on your own. Asking questions shows your genuine interest in your children, and they will recognize all the more that you care when you take the time for regular communication. Really listen to what they are going through as they strive to find friends, meaningful activities, scholastic success, and purpose as they grow up.

It is also a great idea to form blessing traditions around holidays and birthdays. Some families have the tradition of writing a poem to every member of the family to give at Christmas time, while giving special blessings on birthdays can make memorable treasures. Reaching milestone birthdays like ten, thirteen, sixteen, eighteen, and twenty-one can also be opportunities to speak blessings over your children. These take some thought and some effort, usually, but they also work to catapult your children into their futures with greater resolve and a greater respect for living right.

Dream with your kids. The word *education* comes from a Latin word that means, "draw forth." When you ask your kids questions, you draw forth from their well of dreams, hopes, and desires. Talk show host Larry King once said, "I have never learned a thing while I was talking. I realize today that nothing I say today will teach me anything, so if I am going to learn a lot today, I will have to do it by listening, and not by talking." That is great advice for anyone, but especially for parents who want to know their children better!

We need to learn to *eulogize* our children. People tend to eulogize at funerals, telling stories and talking about the qualities that made the deceased so special to them. But why do we wait until it is too late for such talk to do them any good? We need to speak blessings over our loved ones while they are still around! *Eulogy* means literally, "good words." No matter what a person is like, we somehow find a way to say good things about them when they are gone; wouldn't it be better to speak good things into their lives while they are still around?

Remember, too, that no matter what you say about a person, if the only time it is said is when they are not there, they are unlikely to benefit from it. While we should certainly pray for blessings for our children in private, we need to speak blessings over them, as well, when they can hear it and in front of other people. If you are not sure how to do this, consider the seven facets of eulogizing a child or a person:

1. acceptance

2. approval

3. affirmation

4. admiration

5. affection

6. appreciation

7. attention

Now some might object that such praise will go to a child's head and make them arrogant and proud, and there is no question some parents brag incessantly about their children to no one's benefit. The next time something like that is happening, take a minute to listen to what they are saying about their children and see who you think it is really about. You will hear that they won this award or got a certain grade-point average or were inducted into such-and-such club or society. The piano teacher said this or that about them being a prodigy or their coach selected them to be team captain for such-and-such sport, or they scored x number of points, goals, or strikeouts in their last game. If you listen closely, you will hear a lot about accomplishments—which are nice, don't get us wrong—but not so much about character. And you will discover that what they are saying is more to make them look good as a parent than to encourage or edify their child.

Thus, you will notice there is a difference between bragging about your kid—which is to make the parent look good—and eulogizing the child, which is to inspire and make emotional deposits into your child's self-image. And this doesn't mean that you won't have to still correct the child from time to time—after all, "No" is still an important parenting word—but now when you do correct them, you can point back to the character traits you have been eulogizing and use them as examples of your confidence that they are better than their actions. Children who have emotional tanks that have been filled with blessings are much easier to correct and discipline, as a rule, than children backed into the corner by negatives with few options but to come out swinging in self-defense.

SPEAK OVER YOUR CHILDREN IN PRAYER

Because we know all lasting blessings flow out of the spiritual realm into the natural one, we must not only speak positively about our children in their presence, but also in the presence of God in prayer. We know of no better way to bless your children than to pray for them on a regular basis. Here are eight ways to pray for your children habitually. Pray over them and pray truth into them.

1. Pray the Holy Spirit will bring them to Christ early in life. (See Psalms 63:1 and 2 Timothy 3:15.)

2. Pray that God will protect them spiritually, emotionally, and physically. (See John 17:15.)

3. Pray that they will honor and respect people in authority. (See Romans 13:1-3.)

4. Pray for them to desire right relationships and be protected from the wrong kinds of friends. (See Proverbs 1:10-15.)

5. Pray for them and their future mate to be kept pure. (See 1 Corinthians 6:14-20.)

6. Pray that they will learn how to submit to the Lordship of Christ and resist the enemy's assaults. (See James 4:7.)

7.   Pray they will have a hatred for sin. (See Psalms 97:10.)

8.   Pray that they will learn how to walk in the Spirit and not in the flesh. (See Galatians 5:16-25.)

THE BOTTOM LINE

The purpose of speaking edifying words and blessings over our children is to reinforce within them that nothing shall be impossible for them if they team up with God in faith and perseverance. Because we want our children to aspire to great things, we must plant great things in their hearts and nurture them as God directs us. We have to infect them with possibilities and belief that they can accomplish good things. We must coach them through continually applying themselves in their education and activities so that they grow toward their dreams. The results will amaze you.

NOTES

1.   John MacArthur, *Successful Christian Parenting* (Nashville, TN: Word Publishers, 1998), 41.

2.   Bill Gothard, *The Power of Spoken Blessings* (Sisters, OR: Multnomah Publishers, 2004), 62-64.

3.   David Kyle Foster, "Interview: Craig Hill Part 1," Mastering Life, September 1, 2008, http://www.purepassion.us/index.php/mastering-life/articles/miscellaneous/item/33-interview-craig-hill-part-1.

Chapter Twelve

LOVE IS THE THEME

A house is made of walls and beams,
but a home is made of love and dreams. —ANONYMOUS

I (Paul) was reading a story a little while back about a father whose son had left for college. One day the father wandered into his son's bedroom reminiscing. Looking around, he happened to see his son's journal. He had taught his son early to chronicle his thoughts and ideas by writing in it every day. He picked it up, thumbed through it, then got an idea. He took his son's journal into the living room and found his own journal. He found the same day in each book and started comparing what his son had recorded to what he had written. Eventually, he came to a day when he had taken his son fishing. On that particular date, the father had written, "Wasted the whole day fishing." When he looked at the same date in his son's journal, he read, "Went fishing with Dad today. Greatest day of my life."

It's often easy for us as parents to miss the significance of the time we spend with our children. When we are in the midst of living life together, we are focused on different things and interpret events differently. For this father, the day was a waste—a pleasant waste, probably, but still a waste—likely because he made little headway on his goals or assignments for work and kept thinking about them throughout the trip. Kids, as you have probably figured out already, have their own interpretations and values. For the dad, the day was a waste, having accomplished nothing, and probably catching nothing as well. But for the son, the day was priceless. He got to spend the day with his dad.

In our family counseling, we have come to realize that there is a famine of genuine love in our land. Parents say that they love their children—and they may even tell them regularly—but do children feel that love? We need to realize, even on our worst days, what we do speaks louder than what we say.

Over the years we have found that there are four demonstrations of love that our children understand above any others. Though they would probably not list these when they are younger, when they have children of their own, these four things are what they will remember as having made the greatest impact on their lives:

1. the way we disciplined them,

2. the way we were involved in their activities,

3. the way we listened to them, and

4. the way we talked to them.

Very few parents give disciplining their children the forethought you have by reading through a book like this one. By now you should be ready for your children's next "stunt," and have a plan for meeting it with love, correction, and consequences. If you take care of yourself in the process of parenting as well—meaning you do what you need to do to keep from getting frazzled, including getting enough sleep, eating right, taking care of your own attitude and outlook through your spiritual disciplines, etc.—you should be able to handle that discipline session without breaking a sweat. Though they may not appreciate it for some time, they will eventually see the lengths you went to in order to see that such sessions were not only effective, but also positive and nurturing. That is a level of love very few ever experience.

But that is only part of the picture. Plugging in to our kids' lives and doing things together that they enjoy is another way of showing love and making kids know how much they are treasured. We are not the first to say that "love is spelled t-i-m-e." This doesn't just mean being their taxi service either, but plugging in to what they are doing and understanding how to help them enjoy their activities. It also means to be with them in the triumphs, challenges, and failures those endeavors bring. These are "manageable" defeats that can teach our kids a great deal about facing bigger and more costly issues down the road.

I (Paul) remember when I was sitting in my office one day, preparing for a revival meeting in North Carolina that was two days away, when Gretchen came in. She was around fifteen at the time—probably a sophomore in high school. She said, "Daddy, I need to talk to you a moment."

I said, "Sure, Hon, what's going on?"

"Well, I know you are going off for a revival meeting next week, and you're leaving in a couple of days, but I need you to stay home with me this week. I just need you to be here with me."

Of course, my mind went a thousand different directions: *Is she on drugs? Is she pregnant? What's going on? What's happening?* I just couldn't imagine why she was making such a request. So I said, "Well, honey, Dad's got a revival meeting—I can't just cancel it and stay home. It's been scheduled for over a year."

She looked at me somewhat sheepishly and said, "Daddy, I know, but I am asking you to please stay home through this next week. I need you to be here with me."

I couldn't imagine what this was about. I asked, "Is there anything going on?"

"No, sir."

"Did anything happen?"

"No, sir."

"Is anything wrong?"

"No, sir. I just need you to be with me."

So I thought about it. As I did, the Spirit of God spoke to my heart. I called the pastor of the church where the meeting was supposed to be. I told him, "Brother, I'm going to have to cancel this revival meeting. I'm not going to be able to come. I just can't come."

He asked, "What's going on? Are you sick?"

"Nah, I'm not sick, but my daughter came to me and asked me to stay home this week."

He seemed a little panicked on the other end of the line. "Is she pregnant?"

"No," I answered.

"Is she on drugs?"

"No."

"Well, then, what's going on?"

I paused and then truthfully answered, "I have no idea. All I know is she asked me to stay home."

I could tell by his tone of voice that he really didn't think that was a good enough reason to cancel. "And you're going to stay home *just because she asked?*"

I steeled myself against a flood of guilt. "I am," I answered. "The way she approached me; the way she asked me—I am going to stay home."

Then he really let me know what he thought of that. "Well, we've had this meeting scheduled for a year, we have advertisements out—" On and on he went, unloading both barrels.

I realized the difficult position it put him in, so I called a couple of friends and asked if there was any way any of them could get over there and do the meeting for me. I gave the pastor a couple of names of men I would recommend to replace me who could do the meeting, but he wasn't satisfied. He said, infuriated, "I'll never use you again!"

I could only say, "Well, if you feel that way, I understand."

He hung up the phone. I thought that was the last time I would ever speak with him.

However, he called back about a half an hour later and apologized, saying, "I don't understand, but if your daughter needs you, I do understand that you need to be with her."

So I called Gretchen into my office and told her, "Sweetheart, I cancelled my meeting. I'm not going to leave in two days. I'm going to be here with you next week."

She grabbed me and hugged me. She was so happy. We even wept together a little bit. We thanked God together. It was wonderful.

So I cancelled my meeting and stayed home that next week. I made sure that I was home every afternoon when she came in from school, waiting with open arms for her to say, "Boy, Daddy, I am sure glad you stayed." But she didn't. Not one time did she even say, "Glad you stayed home, thank you Daddy for doing that." I lost the income from the meeting, the opportunity to minister to the people, *and nothing happened*. I expected at least a broken arm or a fender bender or something like that, but there was nothing out of the ordinary. As a matter of fact, she just lived her life like nothing was unusual.

If you asked her today, however, "Gretchen, can you go back to any time when your daddy did something special that made you feel he really loved you unconditionally and valued you more than anything else?" she'd go back to this time. She never asked me to do it again, either. I think it was just her way of saying, "I wanted to know I was more important to you than your work or whatever else." I let her know that she was, and it meant a lot to her.

LOVE BY LISTENING DEEPLY

As we discussed in a previous chapter, the everyday practices of how we talk with and to our children also tell them how important they are to us and communicate our love to them. To be well heard is to know you are accepted. To be spoken to politely when you lash out at the other person not only communicates love and respect, but also has a way of quenching hostilities and accessing the heart.

One time we were sitting around the table at our house with the family. Paul Edward was seventeen. I (Paul Sr.) had been traveling a lot, so it was good to be back with the family. We hadn't had a chance to sit and talk together for a long time. I asked Paul Edward what he had done the night before. He said, "None of your business."

Complete silence filled the room. I think Thom turned white with fear of what I would do.

There was a little intense confrontation between Paul Edward and me.

Then Paul Edward snapped. It was the first time that he ever raised his voice at me. He stood up, looked me in the eye, and said, "You're starting to piss me off!"

Everybody around the table froze. I could tell what they were thinking: *Oh my God, Daddy's going to kill him! He's dead! He's dead for sure!*

But in that split second, the Spirit of God got a hold of my thoughts and gently spoke to me. He said, "You can either drive him away, or you can win him."

So, without raising my voice, I said, "Son, do you know how much we love you?" With my past anger issues, normally I would have gone ballistic on him, but I didn't. I said, "Son, we love you. Please sit down. Let's talk about this. Just please sit down. We love you."

Paul melted back into his chair, on the edge of tears, but keeping them in. In the end, it was the most important conversation we have ever had with him, and I don't think it would have ever happened had I not been willing to obey God and respond with kindness instead of anger.

We know it is not easy raising children. Many well-meaning parents provide things for their kids as acts of love; and indeed, what we provide our children is love, but in parental language. Our children don't necessarily see what we provide as loving them, however—to them providing for the family is simply our job. Some of the most loving and emotion-ally content families in the world are those who don't have all of the nice things of life—and oddly, some of the saddest, most unloved kids have been given everything. So if you want your kids to know that you love them, you have to do more than just put a roof over their heads and buy them things and take them places. You have to say it in a language that communicates love—you need to communicate to your children and really listen to them.

CHANGING THE ATMOSPHERE OF YOUR HOME

By now, as you have read through this book, we are sure you have received some new tools and some better ideas for how to raise your children. You are probably more excited about being a par-ent—at least we hope you are—and looking forward to upcoming "learning opportunities."

However, if your kids are no longer infants, don't expect your new plan of action to turn things around right away; nor are your kids going to be so sure you have changed before they see the new you for a period of time. While we have discussed better ways to discipline, commu-nicate with, and teach your children, the "new you" can't just walk in the door one day and expect the kids to sign up for the new program right away. If they have "ruled the roost" for a while, don't expect them to give it up without at least a bit of a fight. Your new perspective and practices are going to take time to bear fruit. If plugging in some of these principles and new methods are going to be very different than what happened in the past, you are going to have to prepare yourself for a bit of a siege.

We suggest that you might want to set a clear demarcation for your family that things are going to be different from here on out—that you want to get a fresh start at being parents. If you feel you need to set a clear, new starting place, the first thing to do is plan out your strategy with your spouse. Make sure you are on the same page for how you will discipline and how you are going to relate to your children. When children feel they are losing control of the home, those little masterminds behind their eyeballs will start playing parents against each other. What will you do if that happens? What are some of the manipulative patterns of behavior you have seen in your kids that the other parent might not have noticed? What area of your children's behavior is a priority to change first? Bedtime? Table manners? Do you feel they should read more and play fewer video games? Do you want them to start learning to play more quietly on their own with the TV off more often? What will be your strategies for empowering them to do that while you cut down on the feedback you don't want?

Once you have all of this started—and this will be an ongoing process, so expect to adjust and modify your plans as you go along—call a family meeting. (By the way, we don't suggest handing your children this book, telling them to read it, and that you will discuss it at dinner on Sunday night! You are going to have to find a way to communicate the coming change in your own way.) Inform your children that you love them dearly, but are not happy about the way the home has been operating as of late. Let them know you have been doing some studying and are planning to make some changes that you want to let them know about. There will be changes that require everyone to make some adjustments and sacrifices—they need to prepare their hearts for them. Let them know that you want their help to make your home a happier, more peaceful place.

Make sure they understand there will be some new standards. Explain clearly what they will be and what the consequences will be for violating them. Make sure that they do not become resentful for suddenly being held to new standards without forewarning—you may even want to develop some of the new standards with them to help them understand their purpose and why everyone will be better off in the long run. They may not understand, but you want to do your best to make sure they know exactly what is coming and why it is happening.

Ask their forgiveness for not having done this sooner so that it would be easier on them. Tell them that there will be some things that work and some that don't, so ask for their patience as you work things out. You as parents are getting used to the new system as well, so it will take some time for everything to settle into a new rhythm. Inform them they can come to you any time if they have concerns or feel they have been wronged. This will give you a fresh starting point and establish the basis for the forthcoming changes.

Then, once you have talked it through with your kids, start to implement your new standards. Go slowly and watch your anger and attitude. Keep in mind that your children are products of your training, whether by intent or neglect, and that these changes are unlikely to be easy for your kids. New training regimens take time and persistence to put into place. (If you have ever tried to implement a new exercise routine for yourself, you will know just how difficult such changes can be!) Remember that retraining is not easy. The repentant parent must remember that the enforcement of new rules can be difficult, because half of the training will be undoing the negative training you have done thus far.

If the children are not learning fast enough, or the training does not seem to be working, then it is time to look for blind spots in your approach, and not time for greater harshness. Children respond best to alert, loving, consistent discipline, not to angry, "don't mess with me kid" parenting.

If you think you really need it, plan for the possibility of several intense days of frequent discipline. You may even consider limiting outside commitments for that time and taking a few days off from work so that you can devote yourself fully to getting things back in order. Some children submit to change easily, but others may not be so willing to adapt. Your kids must learn right away, however, that you are very serious about making a change, and that the reason for it is that you love them too much to let things continue as they were before.

One last thought: keep in mind that most of us find it easier to follow the leadership of someone who likes us. Your children must know that you love them and you are affectionate toward them. Affirm to your children that you love them and have their best interests at heart, and speak hopefully to them about what things will be like with your new standards. No one is really motivated to please someone who thinks the worst of them all of the time, so let your kids know you see great potential in them. Assure them that this is just another part of being sure their futures are bright and their lives in the present are more peaceful and, believe it or not, fun.

THE BOTTOM LINE

You can never assume your children know that you love them. You have to say it and show them. Say the magic words, "I love you," frequently. Every time you say it, another brick is laid in the foundation of their self-image as a lovable person you are proud to say is your child. Get physical with them. Hug your kids, tumble around on the floor with them, cuddle while watching TV together, hold their hand while walking through the mall—teach them through your contact what proper touches are as expressions of affection.

Give them time—not quality over quantity, but quality *and* quantity. One "quality" conversation a day that lasts five minutes isn't enough! Realize, as well, that you will seldom if ever spontaneously find extra time to be with your kids—you must plan it. Move other commitments out of the way to make room. We have lost count of the times that we have shown more respect and love to strangers than to our own family. You need to practice unconditional love where it is the most difficult and with the people you love the most—with the ones you know the best and who know you the best—and you need to do it every day.

Our kids face constant peer pressure, teasing, stress, and temptations. We parents have long forgotten what that can be like, and many of the stresses our kids face weren't even around when we were their age. One of the most loving things we can do is provide a home where our children can rest from those pressures, a place where they are loved and accepted for who they are, and not ridiculed for who they are not. Remember: "God don't make no junk!" Your children are His divine masterpieces, even if He is far from finished with them yet—or with you, for that matter.

Think of it this way: if God had a refrigerator, your picture would be on it; and if He had a wallet, your picture would be in it. So is your child's. If God wrote out His will—and He did—your name would be under "beneficiary," and so would your child's. If God could choose to live anywhere in the universe—and He can—He would choose to live in your heart, as well as your child's heart. You and your children are that important to Him.

Remember the great words about love written by the apostle Paul, and apply them in how you treat your spouse and your children every day:

> *Love is patient, love is kind and is not jealous; love does not brag and is not arrogant, does not act unbecomingly; it does not seek its own, is not provoked, does not take into account a wrong suffered, does not rejoice in unrighteousness, but rejoices with the truth; bears all things, believes all things, hopes all things, endures all things. Love never fails* (1 Corinthians 13:4-8).

The purpose of love is to teach your children that love never, ever fails. Prove this to them every day by the way you treat them, speak to them, and interact with them. There is no better lesson for them to catch from you.

Chapter Thirteen

SINGLE PARENTING

For He Himself has said, "I will never desert you, nor will I ever forsake you," so that we confidently say, "The Lord is my helper, I will not be afraid." —HEBREWS 13:5-6

Divorce can be devastating to children, but with God's help, you are far from alone. If you are a single parent, God's promises have not changed. While we certainly believe that it is best for a child to be raised by a father *and* a mother working together, we also know we have a big God. He will not leave us without help, He will not turn His back on us, and He has never stopped loving us or our children.

Of course, if a family is affected by a divorce, it is not only the children who suffer. As you've heard whenever you travel by plane, if the oxygen masks fall from the ceiling, you must make sure your mask is in place before you help your children. The same principle applies if you find yourself parenting alone. You need to get yourself into a better place before you can help your kids. You can't pull someone from the edge of a cliff if you're hanging on by your fingertips as well. You need to get a grip before you can help your children. You need to secure yourself first—tied firmly to something solid—then you can lower a rope to help the other person. And we have found there is nothing more secure to be tied closely to than Christ Himself.

While staying close to God will make things more manageable, that doesn't mean they will be easy. When there is the loss of a marriage through divorce, there is grief to be worked through just as if a loved one had died, and that is a process that cannot be rushed or forced. Experts tell us that in situations like these, it normally takes around two years to work through the five stages of grief—denial, anger, bargaining, depression, and then acceptance. As a single parent, you need to be doubly sure you are looking after your own attitude and energy, especially during that time, even if you remarry in that window. You can't love and cherish your kids when you feel empty of love and significance yourself. Get the grace you need from God, and then share it richly with your children.

Billie and I want to offer a few suggestions based on God's Word that we believe are important to remember as you work to find better footing for yourself as a single parent. These principles have helped the families we've counseled overcome breakup—and might help you to check up on your own place of security and stability as you facilitate the healing of your own family.

1. Don't blame or shame.

We have never met anyone who can live in any peace as long as they were blaming or holding a grudge against another. When you lose your spouse through divorce, there is going to be some anger and blame. In situations where you have joint custody of the children and have to see each other regularly, there is a great temptation to allow that anger and blame to continue. But you can never be free to move on until you truly forgive. As the old saying goes, "Unforgiveness is like drinking poison and then expecting the other person to die." When we fail to forgive for whatever reason, we hurt ourselves and our children far more than anyone else.

Realize your children will also be dealing with forgiveness issues—and that, however unjustified, they are going to feel to blame in some way. The more you blame and criticize your former spouse in their presence, the more difficult it will be for them to forgive and realize they were never the issue. Now you may believe that you are the innocent victim, but that doesn't make unforgiveness, constant bickering when you are with your former spouse, or speaking badly about them when you're not, any healthier. You may say, "Well, I'm only telling the truth," but you have to ask yourself, "Am I speaking that truth in love?"

I (Paul) recently read a definition of slander that really spoke to me: "Slander is truth told about someone designed to hurt his or her character." If your intention is to make your former spouse look bad in the eyes of your children, you're doing something wrong! Plain and simple! When you slander, you're hurting your children more than anyone else—after all, your former spouse is still their parent. You need to resist using your children as weapons aimed at hurting your ex-spouse. Nothing good will ever come of it.

Not only that, but teaching your children to forgive and love does not have an age distinction. If your children are older when your spouse leaves, it's going to be more difficult for them. Don't add to the burden by playing the blame game. It will only hurt them and ultimately make them think less of you, not the one you're blaming.

Ephesians 5:12 tells us, *"For it is disgraceful even to speak of the things which are done by them in secret."* Normally, children do not know what's gone on in private between you and your former spouse. If your spouse betrayed you, your kids don't need to know the painful details. You'll have to ask God for wisdom on how much to share—although it's always better to be more general than give specifics. Whatever you do, don't shame your former spouse in front of the children or even in private. God knows how to deal with your ex-spouse—that's not your job.

Remember, children will naturally defend their parents, even if it is to the other parent. It's in their DNA to do so. When you criticize your former spouse to them, you force them to take sides, and that is very difficult and unhealthy for them. However, when you act in a godly way, it will reinforce to your children that you're a person of character and integrity, even in hard times. That's a lesson you want them to learn.

2. Be truly forgiving of your former spouse.

The other day Billie Kaye found a definition of forgiveness that has really stuck with us: "Forgiveness is relinquishing your desire to hurt someone who has hurt you." Wow! What a great working definition. You see, sometimes we say that we're hurt for the sake of our children, when in fact it's *we* who have an unforgiving spirit. If we allow seeds of unforgiveness into our hearts, they will grow into bitterness, and bitterness has roots that are very difficult to free ourselves from. Too often we water and fertilize seeds of bitterness in our hearts with what we say and think instead of pulling them up and tossing them away as we should. Bitterness will lock you in a prison, and unforgiveness will hand the key to the jailer.

Your children *need* you to get beyond your hurt and forgive so they can do the same. We didn't say justify or excuse—we said *forgive*. Let it go! Move past it! Bury it and stop digging it up again and again. It's your children's hearts you need to be primarily concerned with. You don't want them to spend most of their adult life the same way you may feel now—untrusting, resentful, hostile, and unforgiving.

Forgiveness is your willingness to bear the consequences of another person's choices. That's exactly what Jesus did for all of us on the cross. He bore the consequences of our choices. It was our choice to sin, and He suffered and died for those sins. So to be like Jesus, we must be willing to bear the consequences of someone else's choices—even if that person is someone who has hurt us very deeply. Children will eventually be forgiving if you are, but the opposite is also true. If you harbor unforgiveness and resentment, so will they. Set your children free by forgiving.

3. *Help establish healthy relationships.*

One of the most difficult challenges if you share custody with your former spouse is to allow your children to cultivate a relationship with their other biological parent without your interference one way or the other. Depending on the age of the children, there can be feelings of shame, abandonment, frustration, hopelessness, *and* despair. To help handle these, they need their own relationship with both parents, even if they now live in different homes. If kids don't find ways to deal with these within their biological family, sometimes they will isolate themselves or run to wrong relationships for the comfort they don't find in either parent.

A children's social worker told us years ago that children never give up hope that their mom and dad will get back together. That's the way God designed them. We realize there are exceptions, however, by and large that is true, even if one or both parents remarry. Children will not stay emotionally healthy through such discordant desires on their own. That's why your role as the primary caregiver is so vital. Your attitude, your heart, and your communication give them the footing they need to establish their own hopes and desires in light of God's best will for them.

So, as long as the courts have seen fit for custody to be shared, it is now up to the parents to not only allow, but also encourage the children to have a healthy relationship with the other parent. There is no question that this can be very difficult, especially if there were past offenses or abuses. Not only that, but despite your best intentions and forgiveness, your ex may be unwilling to forgive and may even try to use your children against you. We have already discussed how damaging that can be for your kids. This puts you in a very tough position, because you really don't have any control over how immature or selfish your former spouse may act. It is definitely a place where you will need God's guidance, and seeking godly counsel from others will help as well. Do not face it alone—pray, get help from your church friends and leadership, and remain an example to your children of emotional health rather than dysfunction. Set boundaries that you can enforce with the other parent to protect yourself and your kids in as loving a way as possible. Remember, you weren't able to "control" your former spouse when you were married to him or her, so you certainly won't be able to control them now.

Healthy communication can never be underestimated. Communication, communication, and more healthy communication is the key to restoration (not snarky remarks or arguing). No matter how many times you have to sit down, take a deep breath, and pray, resolve to communicate honorably. Follow the principles we have already discussed in this chapter and you will have the moral conviction and courage to set strong boundaries to protect the children from being wounded any further. Do everything you can to avoid arguing with your former spouse.

While this is a very tough scenario, the good news is that if your kids have at least one healthy, strong parent showing the right way to behave and forgive, then they are likely to recognize that and choose those behaviors rather than the destructive ones. The older your children are, the more likely they will see what's really going on, but for younger kids, this will take more time. Chances are, it won't even happen while they are still in your home, but you can be assured that if you honor God through such times, He will help your kids understand and make the right choices later. If you remain emotionally positive and forgiving, eventually the truth will emerge, and your kids will be all the better for your example.

4. Being single is better than being married to the wrong person.

Paul the apostle gives us a great admonishment in Philippians 4:6-7: *"Be anxious for nothing, but in everything by prayer and supplication with thanksgiving let your requests be made known to God. And the peace of God, which surpasses all comprehension, will guard your hearts and your minds in Christ Jesus."* What a great promise for a single parent. As we've talked with many single parents, the one desire they have is to find the right mate for them and new parent for their children.

We have seen tragic results time and time again when a single parent married on the rebound. This kind of marriage can be devastating to the children as well as the parent. Waiting for the Lord to bring that right person into your life is always the right thing to do. Being in the right environment to maximize that opportunity is absolutely imperative. Whether in church or business relationships, associate with like-minded and like-hearted people. When you surround yourself with the right kind of people, then those who would not be healthy for you or your child will become apparent. Raising children as a single person will have many challenges, but with the right support in your life you don't need to fear your child being deprived just because you have yet to remarry. Other moms and dads who love you will help love and mentor your children. This may not be the very best, but it's worlds better than the alternative of the wrong spouse.

5. You don't have to be lonely.

Being alone is no fun for most of us. Companionship and fellowship is a very important part of life. We have known married couples who feel very alone and without companionship. This is not an issue isolated to single parents. This is an issue of the emotions and the heart. God even reminds us in Genesis 2 that it's not good for man to be alone. We think women have an easier time being alone in one sense than men. Men are so dependent on their wives for so many things to make life more livable. As self-sufficient as women may be though, there's still an emotional need to be loved, valued, and cared for by a man. There is a certain degree of companionship found in family and friends, but it cannot take the place of a more permanent, more intimate relationship. With some exceptions, I believe that God has designed marriage to fill that deeper need. But even if you're married, the very deepest need of your heart can only be met by Christ Himself. So much of the time we really are, like the song says, "looking for love in all the wrong places." So our suggestion for being lonely is to deepen your relationship with God before you do anything else.

After talking about marriage "being honorable" in Hebrews 13, God said, *"Let your conduct be without covetousness; be content with such things as you have. For He Himself has said, 'I will never leave you nor forsake you'"* (Heb. 13:5 NKJV). God is not speaking against ambition, but simply saying, "Learn to live a contented life and know that I am all you need."

Having great companionship is not the secret to contentment any more than having great wealth. For the Christian, seeking first the Kingdom of God and His righteousness is the beginning (see Matt. 6:33), because God knows what we have need of in every area of life, and He is able to supply us with what He knows is best for us. God is closer than our very breath and is a friend who sticks closer than a brother. Over and over in the Bible, we are reminded that all relationships pale in comparison to our relationship with our Lord Jesus. He is our joy and peace, our friend and lover, and He is our all in all.

6.   *Above all, help your kids grow spiritually.*

As we have discussed previously, Proverbs 22:6 tells us, *"Train up a child in the way he should go, even when he is old he will not depart from it."* When God wanted to "train" His first two children to not touch, He did not place the forbidden object out of their reach. Instead, He placed the *"tree of knowledge of good and evil"* in the *"middle of the garden"* (Gen. 2:17, 3:3). Being in the middle of the garden, they had to walk by it continually. God's purpose was not about protecting the tree; it was about educating Adam and Eve concerning "good and evil." It was about teaching His children that life is a series of choices, good and bad, and both have consequences. When we choose good, we live happier lives—when we don't, we pay the consequences.

In a similar way, your children need moral teaching, especially if they deal with the challenges of life split between two households. That means we need to take—yes, we said *take*, not *send*—them to church regularly so that they receive positive influences from multiple sources. Pray with your kids when you put them to bed; read to them out of the Bible; as they get older have devotional times where you can discuss what you believe and answer their questions. We don't mean hour-long teaching sessions, but maybe ten minutes or so at breakfast or before bed when you read together and talk about God.

Be a moral example to your kids. Keep your home environment healthy and seek out positive, moral influences. By continually reinforcing godly values, your children will learn about the importance of their choices. It will help them grow up to learn accountability, the value of hard work, what practices lead to success and which lead to failure, and that there are rewards and punishments in this life that result from the way we live and the decisions we make.

You will find, as your children grow older, they will treasure your investment in them spiritually. Teaching and training a child to work and be responsible for their choices will yield great fruit in the future. We promise you that the joy you will experience in seeing them grow will go unrivaled in this life.

THE BOTTOM LINE

When a family is broken through a divorce, there is healing that needs to be done that will take time. There is a grief process to work through, and while that is happening, emotions are going to peak much more quickly than they ever did before. Add to this that you are now a single parent, and things can seem very grim. But God is still with us in such situations, and we need to cling to Him and His help as never before.

Don't forget to take care of your own spiritual life and demeanor and don't be afraid to ask for the help or counsel you may need from your local church and fellowships. Trust God to give you wisdom in dealing with both your children and your ex-spouse. Forgive, don't bury your anger or bitterness, and let God make you the whole parent He wants you to be. It will benefit you, your children, and every relationship in your family.

Chapter Fourteen

REBUILDING BROKEN RELATIONSHIPS

It takes one person to forgive;
it takes two people to be reunited. —LEWIS B. SMEDES

Perfect parents—if there are such people—do not necessarily produce perfect children. We live in a fallen world and reality dictates the necessity of dealing with things when they go wrong, despite our best efforts to keep that from happening. Humankind is a fallen race, prone to sin and all of the difficult things that go with it. Therefore, the road back to God is often filled with bumps and potholes. A couple may have three children who seem to be on a rail to success, and then another who goes in exactly the opposite direction. Though we hope and pray this never happens, this can lead to the heartbreak of broken relationships with our children. What do we do when everything with one or more of our children doesn't go exactly as we had hoped?

We are given such a scenario in the Parable of the Prodigal Son found in Luke 15. The second-born son of a certain father rises up and demands his portion of the family inheritance, then he hits the road.

"A man had two sons. The younger of them said to his father, 'Father, give me the share of the estate that falls to me.' So he divided his wealth between them. And not many days later, the younger son gathered everything together and went on a journey into a distant country, and there he squandered his estate with loose living. Now when he had spent everything, a severe famine occurred in that country, and he began to be impoverished. So he went and hired himself out to one of the citizens of that country, and he sent him into his fields to feed swine. And he would have gladly filled his stomach with the pods that the swine were eating, and no one was giving anything to him. But when he came to his senses, he said, 'How many of my father's hired men have more than enough bread, but I am dying here with hunger! 'I will get up and go to my father, and will say to him, "Father, I have sinned against heaven, and in your sight; I am no longer worthy to be called your son; make me as one of your hired men."' So he got up and came to his father. But while he was still a long way off, his father saw him and felt compassion for him, and ran and embraced him and kissed him. And the son said to him, 'Father, I have sinned against heaven and in your sight; I am no longer worthy to be called your son.' But the father said to his slaves, 'Quickly bring out the best robe and put it on him, and put a ring on his hand and sandals on his feet; and bring the fattened calf, kill it, and let us eat and celebrate; for this son of mine was dead and has come to life again; he was lost and has been found.' And they began to celebrate.

"Now his older son was in the field, and when he came and approached the house, he heard music and dancing. And he summoned one of the servants and began inquiring what these things could be. And he said to him, 'Your brother has come, and your father has killed the fattened calf because he has received

him back safe and sound.' But he became angry and was not willing to go in; and his father came out and began pleading with him. But he answered and said to his father, 'Look! For so many years I have been serving you and I have never neglected a command of yours; and yet you have never given me a young goat, so that I might celebrate with my friends; but when this son of yours came, who has devoured your wealth with prostitutes, you killed the fattened calf for him.' And he said to him, 'Son, you have always been with me, and all that is mine is yours. 'But we had to celebrate and rejoice, for this brother of yours was dead and has begun to live, and was lost and has been found.'"(Luke 15:11-32)

The reaction and response of that father to this young man gives us great insight as to how we should respond should we find ourselves in the same situation.

STEP ONE: HONESTLY ASSESS THE SITUATION

Before we can do anything to remedy a situation, we must be willing to honestly ask God to show us what is going on through His eyes, not our own. How does God see each person in the situation? How does redemption play a part in each person's life? What is God's hope and plan for each one? Remember, your growth in this situation is just as important as your child's.

If your goal is to simply reclaim the child, your success is very much at risk. Your goal should be to allow God to cleanse your heart as well as the heart of the child, and that you both gain wisdom, understanding, and character in the process. Accordingly, you must come honestly before God and allow Him to show you the heart of the reale problem. During this process it is vitally important that you seek the counsel of your spouse and possibly other family members as to where you may have failed the child. This is a tedious process and must be tempered with openness, honesty, and willingness to repent. While not every opinion is valid, you must listen with an open heart before you can decide what is true and what should be dismissed; be discerning as to what is most important and what is less so, what is from a skewed perspective, or what are conclusions drawn from incomplete facts. You will need God's help to do this. Jesus exhorted us to first examine ourselves before taking steps to restore another in Matthew 7:3-5:

> *Why do you look at the speck that is in your brother's eye, but do not notice the log that is in your own eye? Or how can you say to your brother, "Let me take the speck out of your eye," and behold, the log is in your own eye? You hypocrite, first take the log out of your own eye, and then you will see clearly to take the speck out of your brother's eye.*

Our recommendation for all parents, especially fathers, is to read John Eldredge's book, *Wild at Heart*,[1] if you have an estranged son. Another great read when a daughter is involved is Angela Thomas' fine work, *Do You Think I'm Beautiful?*[2] These resources will help you move past the surface conflict and find the root problem and source of your struggle.

When relationships are broken, spirits are wounded. It's not until you are honestly willing to examine yourself before the Lord and accept what you find that you will be on the path to recovery. You may find nothing on your part that would account for the deviant behavior of your child. No parent is perfect, but it is also possible that you are not responsible for what has happened. If you are honest with God, He will show you what you need to see. If there is nothing to see, don't make something up and don't nitpick. Some parents will pick themselves apart looking for something simply because they feel that if they can find something in their own lives, they can correct it, and the whole horrible mess will be over. If the problem is you, God wants you to know and will clearly show you what it is. If not, move on. And move on in the confidence and assurance that you can act boldly and decisively with God's backing.

STEP TWO: HAVE THE RIGHT ATTITUDE

Broken relationships with your children generally come in the adolescent and early adult years of their lives. Therefore, it is essential you understand that you cannot command their repentance and reconciliation. Those days are behind you. Now you must earn the right to be heard and be admitted back into their lives. As much as we dislike this idea, it is a reality. They have reached the age where they have to make decisions for themselves.

You can't make a son or daughter love you, and you can't make them accept your point of view. Only they can decide the next step for their lives. If their current life path is part of the issue dividing you, beware the trap of thinking you can make them choose you over their previously chosen direction. In the adolescent years, you may be able to force some superficial compliance, but ultimately they themselves must choose to love you and begin the path of recovery or change. By the time they are adults and out of your home, you have to respect who they are as adults and that coming home for the holidays or to visit is their choice now, not yours.

Your right attitude going into any conversations with them will allow you to listen to their thoughts and hear their point of view without interrupting or letting your own opinions block your understanding. Then you should be able to ask them thought-provoking questions or share life experiences in order to help them understand your point of view. While you cannot drive them back home, you can let them know that the door is open and you will welcome them back with open arms.

Many times, getting a right attitude involves dealing with the embarrassment that a wayward child brings to your family. Shame is a very powerful emotion—some believe it to be our strongest. It is so overwhelming, we will do almost anything to avoid it, and often do so without any conscious thought. Every parent wants to be proud of their children and is subject to humiliation. If a child goes wrong, we feel it to our core. And today's society is loaded with opportunities for parents to feel guilty about the way they raised their children.

There was a time when parents worried about school detention and traffic tickets. Now it is more along the lines of pregnancy, sexually transmitted diseases, drug abuse, or homosexuality. However, we must remember that as parents, this embarrassment should be momentary. It will go away if we will confront it, while your child could bear the scars of his or her mistakes for a lifetime. Repentance and reconciliation will overpower embarrassment every time—and it will make all of the difference in your child's life and your relationship with that child. There is much more at stake than you avoiding embarrassment, especially if your child stands on the brink of forfeiting great potential and plunging into a lifetime of suffering.

A right attitude also requires that you trust God to turn the heart of your child. You must refrain from trying to do God's work for Him. This means being careful to stay away from little cutting remarks, nagging, or badgering your child about their issues when you are together. Attempts to bully or manipulate your young adult child will only push him or her farther away. You must not play the victim, either, and try to make the child feel bad or sorry for all that you are suffering. This just makes your child's own suffering that much more difficult to bear and conveys that your concern is more for yourself than for your son or daughter.

STEP THREE: DISCERN THE PROPER RESPONSE

Most broken relationships with children come as the result of some form of rebellion, whether provoked or not. However, there are exceptions to that. If we look at Luke 15, we will see that there are two other parables associated with the one about the prodigal son, and Jesus delivered them sequentially as part of the same message to those He addressed. It is worth looking at all three together to better understand what He was trying to say.

The first is the Parable of the Lost Sheep. The sheep was lost because it simply wandered away. So the shepherd left the flock and went to retrieve the one lost wanderer. In his book *Parenting Prodigals*, Phil Waldrep calls this an intellectual prodigal.[3] At the root of the problem is the child's lack of knowledge or giving in to deception. In this case, the child is still approachable, especially if the child is younger, and with the proper attitude, can be corrected or brought back to the truth relatively easily.

It should go without saying that your approach is going to be the key. When you approach your child, he or she must sense your absolute acceptance and respect for his or her right and ability to think independently. You will get nowhere mocking or belittling your child's thoughts or beliefs. If you can accept the child where he or she is by conveying your love and acceptance, you'll be able to guide him or her toward change. That doesn't mean that you must accept your child's error, but you must not attack your son or daughter personally when you confront the error. For example, you must never refer to the belief as being "stupid" or "dumb." Those words will be received as a reflection of the one who holds the belief rather than the belief itself. Now you have insulted your child as a person and defensive walls will go up! Once the insults are out, in order for your child to abandon error and embrace truth, it is no longer just a matter of leaving one idea and choosing another, but your child must also agree with you that he or she was stupid or dumb to have embraced that line of thinking in the first place. You have just greatly reduced your chance of success. Instead, respect your child's thoughts, treat your child as the young adult he or she is, and then present your carefully thought out case for the truth, appealing to your child's spirit, logic, and conscience.

The second parable has to do with a lost coin. Money is never lost on purpose. This is a relationship broken as the result of carelessness or something done accidentally. It can happen when either person, parent or child, acts carelessly or foolishly. It can be your kid's first detention at school, or it can be your failure to show up at a little league game. It can be your broken heart or the child's wounded spirit.

Proverbs 18:19 tells us, *"A brother offended is harder to be won than a strong city, and contentions are like the bars of a citadel."* There are several ways to get into a highly fortified city, but none are easy. You may attempt to climb the wall, but we have already established the fact that you cannot force this issue. You can starve them out, but don't count on that tactic changing a heart. Or you can wait for an unexpected opening in the wall that will allow you the opportunity to demonstrate genuine love and care that will once again open his or her spirit to you.

We were once told the story of frustrated parents who were faced with their son's failing grades in college. His first year saw him on the Dean's List with a very high GPA, but the second year his grades began to steadily decline. They had done all they knew to do from scolding to threatening. Nothing seemed to work. Their efforts just drove him farther away. Word came that he had been placed on academic suspension, and they were furious.

Fortunately, they sought counsel from a wise pastor who helped them see that perhaps God was making some changes in the direction of their son's life. As the son came home from school braced for a fight, his heart was melted as his parents voiced their concern and reaffirmed their love saying, "We know this failure has hurt you and is embarrassing for you. We just want you to know that we love you and we feel that God may be preparing you for a change of direction in your career and future." The young son left the room that day with renewed determination to use his time of suspension to prepare to return to school and finish, making his parents proud. However, that never happened. During his time at home, God changed everything from his relationship with his parents to his intended career path. When he returned to school, it was to prepare for the ministry, which he did successfully.

There is another sequence that is common in broken relationships that falls under the Parable of the Lost Coin. It happens when a parent deeply hurts a child, whether in carelessness, simplicity, or just insensitivity. It can happen when a promise is not kept, an expectation is not met, or something is done on the part of a parent that embarrasses or humiliates the child. It is an offense that, for whatever reason, has gone unforgiven on the part of the child and the child's spirit has now closed toward the parent in bitterness. When this happens, the offending parent must be willing to take the necessary steps to reopen that spirit as they gently approach the child and inquire about the problem. Once the child is willing to share the problem, the only viable course of action for the parent is to ask for forgiveness. No justification. No excuses. Just ask for forgiveness. You may feel that you are innocent or that the whole thing is petty, but it's real to your son or daughter, and it hurt deeply enough to cause a rift. Perception is reality in the mind of the offended. The only thing that can correct it is sincere apology and forgiveness.

The third situation found in Luke 15 is, of course, that of the prodigal son. This son left in rebellion prompting a totally different response on the part of the father. Just as it does in childhood, rebellion requires an approach unlike any other situation. In childhood, it requires chastening, and that is the responsibility of the parent. In adulthood, it requires chastening that comes from God. The father in this parable knew that if he denied his son his inheritance the boy would have stayed in the home, remained rebellious, and been a source of trouble, possibly corrupting the whole house. So he made a very difficult decision and allowed the son to leave, turning him over to God and allowing Him to deal with the boy's rebellion. You see, God has a built-in cure for rebellion. It's the natural consequences of our actions. Skilled parents will always allow a rebellious child to reap the natural consequences of their actions. Although it is perfectly fine for a parent to rescue a normally obedient child from the consequences of a foolish mistake, the natural consequences of a rebellious act are the teaching class- room of God and should not be interfered with by parents. Parents who do so, ultimately become the enablers of the child's sin and delay God's plan for the child's restoration.

This father didn't make the mistake of interfering with the con- sequences of his son's decisions. He allowed his son to step out from under his authority—he had already taken himself out anyway—and onto the pathway of God. Being totally unprepared for life, the boy squandered away his inheritance. No problem, he thought, "I'll just get a job." What he didn't understand was that he was now dealing with God as his disciplinarian. God responded by saying, "Can you spell f-a-m-i-n-e?" (my paraphrase). So the land was struck with a famine and the young man found himself wrestling pigs for some- thing to eat. I've always thought this to be a bit of divine irony: a Hebrew boy landing in a pigpen.

When God takes you down, He takes you all the way down in ways that could not be accomplished by anyone else or by any other set of circumstances—and He does it with infinite skill, eternal wisdom, and unconditional love. It was here that the young man experienced a brokenness in his heart that only God could inspire. When he came to himself, home was where he wanted to be. So he went back to his family a new man, humble of spirit, and anxious for the embrace of his dad.

STEP FOUR: FIGHT FOR CHILDREN WHILE THEY ARE AWAY

Whether your children are in the home or not, communicating with you or not, you can always fight for them while they are away by ear- nestly praying for them. In fact, as parents, we hold the best position in the Kingdom of God to do just that. In Ephesians 6:12, the apostle

Paul explained, *"Our struggle is not against flesh and blood, but against the rulers, against the powers, against the world forces of this darkness, against the spiritual forces of wickedness in the heavenly places."* The battle is won in Heaven first, and then on the earth. A family crisis of this nature should always improve your prayer life. Don't be shy about approaching God. If your prayer life hasn't been what it should in the past, or you know that there is sin in your life, go to God boldly and deal with it. This is God's call for you to fix things. Clean your act up by repenting of past failures, and then go to God with confidence. As the writer of Hebrews tells us, *"Therefore let us draw near with confidence to the throne of grace, so that we may receive mercy and find grace to help in time of need"* (Heb. 4:16).

Begin by praying for the things that you know are wrong. Then continue by listening for God to prompt you as to how to pray specifically for your son or daughter. Those promptings may come in the form of thoughts as you pray or think about the situation, or they can come as you read books or Scripture, hear a message at church or on the radio, or as you listen to your spouse or a wise friend or counselor as they share their thoughts and experiences. You don't have to tell God how to save your child; He can figure that out for Himself. Just make sure you don't stop praying, listening, then praying again over what you hear, and doing exactly what He tells you to do.

STEP FIVE: PREPARE FOR THE CHILD'S RETURN

Parents should always watch for and expect the return and reconciliation of estranged sons and daughters. The Bible says that as the prodigal son returned, his father saw him while he was still a long way off. (See Luke 15:20.) This happened because the father was looking for and anticipating his return. The son had prepared a speech for his dad when he got home, but the dad had also prepared for that day.

Notice as well that the father didn't lecture the returning son on all that he had done wrong. There was no need for that. God had delivered to him a brand-new son. He simply welcomed him home and reinforced his identity in the family. (See Luke 15:22-24.) As symbols of this, the father gave him a ring, a robe, and some shoes. Of these, Phil Waldrep writes:

> The best robe in the house was reserved for an honored guest. The ring signified that his position of sonship, which he forfeited when he left, was being reinstated. Sandals were worn by family members; slaves went barefoot.[4]

Then the fatted calf was slain and a fellowship meal was prepared. The past was past, and the future was ahead to be embraced.

A PERSONAL EXAMPLE

Family vacations and such are everyone's best memories. We always went someplace different each year as the children were growing up—Niagara Falls, the Mohican Trail, Navarre Beach. We got off with our family by ourselves. It is a tradition we have continued. For the past twenty years now, even with them grown, every other year we have given our children and their spouses a free vacation for all of us to share together. We pay for everything plus give them spending money. We have been to Manzanillo, Mexico; Hawaii; Possum Kingdom Lake; and several other great places. We intend to continue this tradition as long as we're alive.

The reason we do this is because we want our families to grow closer as we all get older. These vacations give us an opportunity for conversations that can't happen at any other time. It gives us the opportunity to speak into our children's marriages and talk about the little foxes—the little issues—that can build up and cause division in a family. We ask them to give us dedicated time each day so that we can watch videos on marriage together or talk. One time we watched a teaching series on *The Five Love Languages*; other times we've watched other series. We pray with them and create an atmosphere where they can talk about challenges with us and with each other.

We have some ground rules for these sessions: no one can get angry, no one can leave the room mad, no one can raise their voice, and no one can accuse. We are there to communicate and resolve concerns with each other. It is not simply to regulate behaviors to make things more tolerable for a time, but to resolve issues that divide us as a family. We encourage repentance, forgiveness, and moving on in love together. We find that all of our relationships tend to come out stronger after these times away together.

The first time we ever did this, we spent a day talking about me (Paul) as their father and the challenges they had growing up. Because I was gone a lot, and I was young and didn't know better, I was very hard on them. I also had a pretty serious temper. Despite how difficult it was to hear what they had to say, it was good for me to receive all of it and not get defensive, which a lot of parents do, and I certainly felt like doing at times. I bit my tongue, though, and listened.

If you are going to communicate with your children, you can't get defensive, and you can't get offended. The minute you do, the communication is over. Your children will clam up. They will say no more, especially if they respect you.

Once I heard them out, I let our kids know how sorry I was, and I asked their forgiveness. Thankfully, they granted it, graciously. I remember after the children shared their hurts and disappointments with me, I asked if they'd like to share their disappointments about their mom. They simply looked at me and said in unison, "What disappointments? She's perfect."

I remember telling them, "Hey, I'm paying for this whole thing; the least you could do is come up with a few lies about your perfect mom." We all had a good laugh, knowing relationships were further repaired.

So, you see, I have some experience with these five steps to repairing relationships with my family, and it has made all the difference in the world to our times together since then. We have wonderful children, but had I never repented, we would never have become as close with them and our grandchildren as we are today.

THE BOTTOM LINE

When there is healing that needs to take place in a family, it is the parents' job to see that it happens, and they have to do it with humility and grace. They need to initiate the conversation, listen actively and empathetically, and then openly discuss the root issues and be willing to ask for or grant forgiveness as is required. Because severe rifts between parent and child rarely happen from a single action, it may take some time to repair. Be prepared to be patient. If the child is older—a teen or even a young adult—you need to be willing to present your case, ask or express forgiveness, and then leave the next step in your child's hands to decide how to respond.

When you go into something like this, you have to be so confident that things are in God's hands and that He will heal hearts. The family, after all, was His idea, and He is still all about healthy relationships. If you do your part, He will do His, and chances are you can share healthier family relationships for years to come, just as we are experiencing.

NOTES

1.   John Eldredge, *Wild at Heart* (Nashville, TN: Thomas Nelson Publishers, 2001, 2010).

2.   Angela Thomas, *Do You Think I'm Beautiful* (Nashville, TN: Thomas Nelson Publishers, 2003).

3.   Phil Waldrep, *Parenting Prodigals* (Baxter Books, 2001).

4.   Ibid., 25.

Chapter Fifteen

FEEDBACK FROM THE TSIKA CHILDREN

Live so that when your children think of fairness, caring, and integrity, they think of you. —H. JACKSON BROWN JR.

Over Thanksgiving of 2012, our family gathered together at the ranch, and we took some time to sit down with our three children to talk about parenting and what it was like for them growing up in our home. At that time, Gretchen was forty-five years of age and had been married for twenty-five years. She and her husband, Mark, have three daughters. Paul Edward ("Paul E." in the questions and answers below) was forty-three and had been married for twenty-four years. He and his wife, Melanie, have two sons and two daughters. Our youngest, Thom, was forty. He and his wife Kelley have a son and two daughters. When all three generations gather around our main table, it is quite a celebration indeed!

We are very proud that our children have grown up wiser than we were as parents, and that they have done such a great job raising our grandchildren. When we asked them about their pasts and their views about being raised in our home, we were surprised at how much we learned. Here is a summary of what proved to be a very energetic and educational question-and-answer session.

Question #1: What are a few of your greatest regrets from growing up in our home?

PAUL E.: One of the things I regret most is missing the opportunity to make more out of myself when I was a teenager. If I could go back and use the brain that I have now, I would utilize it more. I would think before I spoke. I know I often spoke unkindly to Mom, and looking back, I wish I had acted more respectfully. I also wish I had paid more attention in general to everything around me—school, family, etc.

GRETCHEN: I wanted to better understand why we believed as we believe. I grew up believing as you did, but when I was cornered, I didn't really know why I believed as I did. Why should I do my devotions daily, pray, go to church all the time, things like that? We were in church all the time, but when I left home, I was surprised how little of the Bible I really understood. Plus, I don't really think that is for the churches to do—it is up to the families to have those kinds of discussions.

PAUL E.: Yeah, that reminds me of my "drug" problem as a teenager: I got *drug* to church Sunday morning, *drug* to church Sunday night, and *drug* to church Wednesday night. Every conference that came through town or was close to us, I got *drug* there.

THOM: The fact that we had to go to church every time the doors were open really made me hate religion until I was in my thirties and better understood what it meant to be a Christian for myself. I would have rather had the one-on-one time of learning, like Gretchen said, than being drug to church all the time with the expectation for the church to teach me everything. Not that we don't take our kids to church and make them go even when they don't want to, but we talk with them more about it, and it feels different now than it did then.

BILLIE: If kids are "marred" by religion in their teens, it takes them some time to get over it. One of the things I regret most is we did not allow our kids to voice their opinions, because we were afraid they would be different from ours. For some reason, we thought—without thinking, really—that if they never expressed a different opinion, they would just grow up thinking as we do! But how do you change opinions if you never give your children a chance to express them and think them through with you? Parents who listen to their kids rather than just sitting around communicating with their peers not only have richer relationships, but also think more alike, because they have debated ideas through, together. How can your kids learn from your wisdom if you never share it on a level playing field? Otherwise, you are just preaching to them.

PAUL SR.: I don't regret having drug the kids to church every time the doors were open, but what I do regret is not spending the time with them privately and personally like Gretchen talked about to teach them out of the Bible and to do that consistently. Not only that, but I wish we had provoked them to dig into the Bible for themselves. Is it a parent's responsibility to take their children to church or to teach their children? That's the real deal. If it's to take them to church, a lot of parents do their job—just taking them to a building. But, if it's about teaching them what we believe, why we believe it, and this is how it is implemented in our lives on a day-to-day basis—whether the children are home schooled, public schooled, or whatever—then I think very few parents actually do that. We'd have had a less bumpy road as a family, if we had spent more time together talking.

Question #2: What angered you and caused you the most resentment?

GRETCHEN: I think it was the legalism during my teenage years, mostly. I didn't like Dad being gone all the time or the "no pants" phase. I hated wearing those culottes, which were the only option for me other than wearing a dress. I also didn't like never being able to have an opinion. I know I needed to be disciplined, but I still resented it. I wish I had just had more chances to talk with Mom about things—I think I would have been less rebellious, if I had had that.

PAUL E.: I think my biggest issue was being humiliated in front of other people—it made me feel stupid—or not really being paid attention to when I was trying to tell Dad something. Dad had this look like he was thinking, "Did you just fall off the stupid truck?" It made me feel so small.

The only thing I wanted to do as a teenager was make my dad proud of me—that was the height; that was it. If he told me to run, I would try to run 1,600 miles an hour, just to make him happy. I remember one time when we were younger he said something to a friend's dad like, "Oh boy, those boys can run!" My friend and I would be out there five minutes later running as fast as we could, just to see if we could get more accolades and approval.

When I was disciplined and confronted, face to face, in front of people, oh my God! That is one thing I have tried not to do with my kids, my boys especially.

PAUL SR.: You are right. The worst thing a parent can do is humiliate or try to intimidate or manipulate their children in front of other people—especially to humiliate them in front of guests or at church when other parents are watching.

PAUL E.: Not to be focused on when I was talking was very frustrating. I often felt like my parents were on another planet. I resented that. It has taught me to look my children in the eyes when they talk to me. I try not to let anything else get in the way of listening to them.

Question #3: How did you handle Dad being away so much?

PAUL E.: Dad was gone a lot from as young as I can remember. Because of that, I didn't know there could be a different way. So, it wasn't a big deal for me. It was just life as I knew it. I never really thought a thing about it. It just made me so much more grateful when he was home. It was fun to see him actually home. But he had to do it. He set the foundation that we have now as a family, and we wouldn't be doing this book if he hadn't done that back then.

GRETCHEN: I had a hard time with it. A daughter's relationship with her dad is so important. For me, with my girls and Mark, it is so important. My brothers may have a different perspective, I don't know. I think a dad molds, for the most part, what kind of man his daughter is going to marry. For me, when Dad was gone, I missed the relationship with him, because I didn't have a very strong one with Mom. My brothers had one with Mom, but I didn't. I wasn't even sure Mom liked me from the time I turned thirteen until I got married. A big part of that was because of my attitude; I will totally take responsibility for that. I was not a nice person. I know I was very inwardly rebellious.

I knew Mom loved me, but I didn't think she really liked me, because it always seemed to be about the boys. I knew Dad liked me. When Dad came home, he took me out of school, and we did stuff together. I don't know if he did that with the boys or not. I'm not mad about it now, but I did miss spending more time with Dad.

BILLIE: I think Gretchen felt I didn't like her because I had to be the disciplinarian when Paul was gone. When he got home, he didn't like to discipline, because he didn't want that to be the first interaction he had with his children.

I think if I had known, I would have done things very differently with Gretchen. I was still so young, living in my own world, so wrapped up in my life and what I was doing. I was more concerned about that than my kids. I didn't even realize that Gretchen felt alone. All I knew was, if she did something wrong, I had to discipline her rather than sit and talk with her and say, "Tell me what is going on. Let's talk about this." My mother certainly never did that with me, so I didn't know how do to that. I am sure I didn't pass that on to Gretchen. This is where communication breaks down in the family—I didn't even know until today that Gretchen felt that way!

PAUL SR.: I think the reason the boys didn't miss me was because of what Billie did. When fathers feel like they are called to do something and have to spend time being gone, the mothers are the ones who set the environment and the atmosphere for the children. They can make it either a positive or a negative situation by what they say and how they act about him being away. It is either, "He is building us a future," or undermining and resentful.

PAUL E.: What a mom does bleeds into the DNA of the children, positive or negative. It would have been different had Dad been home for ten years and then started to travel after that, but as it was, we didn't know life could be any different from the time we were old enough to think about it.

THOM: The reason I got off the road after being on the golf circuit was because I saw breakdowns start to happen in my family. Kelley was supportive and everything was fine, but it had to come to an end. It was just getting to be too much, especially when Kadie came along, and it wasn't helping that I was gone all the time. So I stopped traveling so much and found a job closer to home.

PAUL SR.: So what are some of the things that you can do to let your children know that you love them *and* like them? To help them be the person God wants them to be? There was no mentorship in our lives on how to raise children beyond the three favorite words of our parents' generation: "No!" "Don't!" "Stop!"

We have to *love* our kids, and that comes naturally, but to *like* them is more dependent and conditional. Kids can think you don't like them because you reject things about them like how they want to dress or what they like or dislike.

BILLIE: I think that feeling of not being liked probably wouldn't have happened if I had let Gretchen feel safe to speak her mind. I know none of the kids felt safe to speak their minds. They knew if they spoke out, they would be in bad trouble.

I don't even remember treating the boys any different. However, that is how I made Gretchen feel.

Question #4: What is your opinion on spanking?

PAUL E.: I am of the opinion—which not everybody shares—that corporal punishment works, if done in love. Dad had a real passion for driving rebellion from us; there is no question. He felt it was his duty and calling to drive it from us, and let me tell you, I am no different. But I have learned that in disciplining my kids, I am not going after their bottoms, I am going after their hearts. I am not looking for behavior modification; I am looking for a heart change. Because of that, I have learned never to discipline in anger.

THOM: I don't ever remember being disciplined by Mom when she was angry, but I don't ever remember being disciplined by Dad where he was loving. Not one time. I was probably twelve or thirteen when I got my last spanking. That was probably a little late to still be spanking your child.

PAUL SR.: It took me some time to learn balance. Thankfully, our children have all balanced out the edification and education with the corporal punishment. Their mother and I did too much of the latter and not enough of the former.

GRETCHEN: I believe that I definitely needed to be spanked up to a certain age. But after that, things needed to change. What age to stop depends on whether it is a mother to a daughter or a father to a son, too. I think moms need to stop spanking their sons sooner, but at the same time, it will be different with each child.

THOM: I think you're right. It totally depends on the child.

BILLIE: All I knew when our kids were growing up was punishment; I didn't understand discipline. I didn't know how to talk with them and teach them that they don't do this or that. All I knew was to get the rod and spank them for doing wrong. Now, I believe rebellion should be punished, not just doing something wrong. Carelessness still requires consequences, but they should be more natural—more about fixing what was broken or things like that.

PAUL SR.: The Word of God says, "*They have transgressed; they have rebelled.*" Transgression is crossing over the line; rebellion is unwillingness to step back in line. So it is a point of rebellion when God deals with us severely, not a point of transgression. He tries to coach us and woo us and love us back into conformity to His will and purpose. But it is when we cross the line and refuse to get back in line that God disciplines.

But just like God, too, I want parents to err on the side of grace rather than legalism. I think that if we can reason with our kids about why they didn't stay within the fence, at that point, and they stay within the fence from then on, we have accomplished something. But if they keep going over the fence, that means they are rebelling.

Paul E.: To add to that, I don't think kids should be disciplined for checking the fence line. I set up fences and boundaries, and I don't discipline them for checking the limitations. That is a natural thing to do—even adults do that in their jobs. It's when you go to cross over the fence that discipline and a level of punishment needs to come into play.

When punishment needs to be involved—pain has to be involved. That could be physical pain, like from a spanking, or emotional pain, like being grounded from television or texting, or for a younger child, having to sit in the corner and miss playtime. If you study the way the brain works, behavior is set up in tracks, and you can actually see thought patterns lined out like roadmaps in your mind. When children do the same thing over and over and over, it cuts a groove and a behavior pattern in the mind—it cuts a clear highway, and if they keep crossing over that fence back and forth, it creates a track and a deep groove of behavior in their lives—it's a definite habit or pattern. Science says the only thing that can change that road from that point forward—to start a brand-new path or road— is pain. Instantaneously, when pain enters into that situation to curb that behavior, it clears the track in front of it to give a clean slate for the parent to realign the behavior. If parents punish their children, but there are no painful consequences, then the track continues on. There's no break in the track for the parent to change the behavior.

PAUL SR.: The question would be then is all pain physical pain? Because, there is pain for an adult in making wrong choices, and there is the pain of the consequences of one's choices. Physical pain is more appropriate for children, as that is the most direct way to halt the behavior. For a teenager, it may be taking their cell phone away or their texting privileges, their Internet access, their ability to do extracurricular activities, their cars, something like that. As they get older, they should have consequences more directly related to what they did—if that is possible. Otherwise, privileges should be lost for irresponsible behavior or poor choices, just as would happen for us as adults.

Question #5: What do you do when a grown person comes to you and says something about your child?

PAUL E.: Wow, that is a great question. I would have to say it depends on the track record of that child.

GRETCHEN: It depends on who the adult is, as well. When our kids were younger, we had a tendency to believe the adults over the kids. But we would talk to them to find out, 1) what made them do it if they did do it? And 2) we would pray that the Lord would reveal what they did wrong to them and talk to them about it. You have to be careful, though. Kids know how to manipulate you and make you feel sorry for them, even when they are guilty.

THOM: If the kids are younger, I trust what the adult said—period. The end. I don't believe younger children are capable of making the proper decisions about taking responsibility for their actions yet. I would explore it if it wasn't a trustworthy adult, but for the most part, I won't side with the child.

Questions #6: What were the things that encouraged you to be a better child?

PAUL E.: Affirmation: edification of who I am and who I was, and knowing and being told I had worth and value. That was the greatest thing for me. I remember the day when Dad called me in—it was late and I hadn't made curfew; I was like sixteen or seventeen—and he said, "Hey son, I am not going to put a curfew on you any longer. You are growing up. You need to be able to make some of your own decisions. All we ask is that you let us know where you are going and who you are with, and that you come in at a reasonable hour." I remember that conversation—it is still crystal clear for me. I was like, "Wow, my dad believes I can make decisions here. He trusts the fact that I am going to make the right call." And I believe there was only one time after that that I had to call him—Bryan Swift and I were in Gulfport cruising and it was 11 or 11:30, and we had finally found the cruising spot. I called Dad and said, "Hey, do you mind if I stay a little bit later?" And he said, "No problem." That was trusting me, and that made me feel like I was smarter and had value and could make good decisions. That was a big thing for me.

GRETCHEN: The discipline did help, and then the freedom when I started driving to not have to account for every place that I was going. Mom and Dad trusted me to be able to make some decisions.

THOM: I would say the same thing. Affirmation was a big thing for me, too.

Question #7: Did any part of buying you things—like the Volkswagen or the truck—was there any part of that that made you want to be better?

THOM: Yes, I liked receiving gifts. It was a big affirmation. And I've got at least one child whose love language is gifts—and he loves giving things.

PAUL E.: It was big for me, too. When our parents would take us to buy clothes or things for us, I felt like we were grateful for that. Besides, they didn't like it when we were ungrateful—it really hurt them. I think that was a big affirmation of us.

GRETCHEN: I don't think the gifts made a big difference for me. For me it was more getting quality time. When Dad would spend time with me when he came home, especially during my teenage years, that made me want to behave better.

I do remember a couple of the best gifts. One was on my thirteenth birthday, when I got to get my ears pierced. I had been asking for years to get my ears pierced and they never let me. I remember Mom picking me up from school and taking me to the mall—and Mom didn't take me to the mall a lot—when we went, we usually went as a family. I was thinking, "What are we doing?" We walked in and I asked, "Where are we going?" And she said, "Well, your dad said you could get your ears pierced." Oh, my gosh, that was like amazing! I loved that!

So for me, though, I don't believe it was the receiving of gifts so much as it was spending quality time together. I just want to spend time with people, and I wanted to spend time with my parents.

Question #8: What are some of the best memories that you have?

THOM: Family vacations. I remember all of them. I don't necessarily remember who was standing next to me when we saw Niagara Falls or the Grand Canyon or the Sequoia trees or whatever, but I remember being together and going to all those places as a family.

PAUL E.: I have two great memories. The first was sitting in a freezing deer stand with Dad on doe day in Clinton, Louisiana. We had climbed up between these two trees, and a doe ran by and Dad didn't shoot her, and I was like, "Dude, what are we out here for? I'm freezing!" But, I remember that because we were together and out hunting, which I still love to do today. Dad and I hung out in the deer stand. That was cool!

My other fondest memories were during the Bible conferences when we had people over—Mom and Dad let me invite friends over—and we would sit at the dinner table listening to the adults talk. I felt so important sitting with the conference speakers.

Despite any negatives, I cannot imagine having a greater childhood. I want my children to have such experiences! I want my kids to look back and say, "Man, we had a great childhood!"

PAUL SR.: It's the quality time; it's the focused attention on being together as a family. Doing special things with your children—making special times. We didn't do enough of it. I remember when we started taking vacations that we didn't have much money, but the kids didn't know that.

PAUL E.: I can tell you right now, I enjoyed that more than anything else. I enjoy getting away with my family like that. I enjoy that so much.

GRETCHEN: My best memories are like Thom's—vacation times. I remember our vacations; I remember the things we did on them. I remember spring breaks. I remember the time Paul and Thom and I got so sunburnt we lay on that bed in that room at Navarre beach. We were all completely red and so burnt, none of us could move.

But we looked forward to those times! At least, I did. The tent revivals, summer vacations, the Bible conferences—even though I regret now that I didn't listen more—my kids have not had experiences like that the way I wish they had.

Personally, though, some of my best memories are when Daddy would come home and he would wake me up at ten o'clock at night, when Mama was still in bed, and we would watch M.A.S.H. together. So when he was home, that was my thing, with Dad, that was our time together that was just the two of us. It was the only real time I got Dad to myself.

Question #9: Do you think your parents are better grandparents than they were parents?

PAUL E.: I think I speak for all of us when I say, "Definitely, but—" They are much more people of grace now, and show their love more than they did when we were growing up. We knew they loved us, but they didn't really show it like they do to our kids. They still have some of the same tendencies. Mom is still a straight arrow and a disciplinarian. Dad still gets upset about little things that are not really that important or meaningful. However, they communicate so much better and there is more education and understanding. It seems to come to them more naturally as grandparents than it did as parents.

THE BOTTOM LINE

The point of asking these questions was to give you all hope. Like the quote from our friend Ron Dunn at the beginning of the book, "The problem with raising children is, by the time you're experienced, you're unemployed." This is why we all make much better grandparents. Like us, you will make mistakes and the way you think will change. But if you will listen, love, and be patient, before and after your children are grown, you'll do great.

CHILDREN

BY PAUL E. TSIKA

Raising children is an easy task
When your heart's in the right place.
And they know you want what's best for them
Because you demonstrate grace.

Oh, there are times you want to pull your hair
And shake your head with doubt,
But as you help them though those times
You learn what love's about.

Your task is clear to raise them well,
To help them grow in years
And honor God with the gift He gave
Even through a river of tears.

A family bonds together in life
In the good times and the bad;
And the memories, love and forgiveness
Will prove the best times that you had.

You must love them unconditionally
And remember what we say;
For God will give the strength you need
So you'll never regret one day.

Chapter Sixteen

THE DAY THEY GET MARRIED

For this reason a man shall leave his father and his mother, and be joined to his wife; and they shall become one flesh.—GENESIS 2:24

As we said in the beginning pages of this book, Psalm 127 tells us that children are a heritage of the Lord—they are a gift from God. The people they are when they leave home is a testimony about who we are as people, as parents, and as Christians. They are the living epistles we have written to the world about who we are, what we believe, and what we teach. We don't want to raise robots—and neither does our Father in Heaven. He wants us to raise children who will choose to honor Him as well as their parents.

Whenever I (Paul) perform a wedding, I give a talk to both sets of parents before the father gives the bride away. I tell them, "Today, you are unemployed. Your parenting ends here. You'll always be their parents; you will always be Mom and Dad, and they are always to honor you as Mom and Dad, but your parenting days have come to an end when you give your child to another. However, your life of mentorship begins. Now you are there to support them, to coach them, to mentor them. Your wisdom can add value to the quality of their lives together, and eventually in their parenting. You will want to stay available to them as parents, but now it is up to them to call and ask for your advice—or not." Then I emphasize, "You, as parents, can be a great source of stress or blessing. It's your choice. I pray you choose to be a blessing."

In addition to this, there are four things that I encourage them always to remember:

1) *Never take sides.*

Taking sides of either your child or his or her spouse will divide the hearts in a marriage, and it will also divide the parents' hearts as well. A house divided against itself cannot stand. Never take sides. The young married couple will go through challenges. They are going to have struggles. They are going to face opposition to their marriage. As their parents, we have to be mature enough to sit down with them and mentor them and share with them, from a biblical perspective, how to work through what they are facing—but only if they ask. They are adults now and are responsible for their own decisions. Never take sides—it will divide their hearts, your hearts, and their home.

2) *Unasked-for counsel is always unwanted counsel.*

Both of our sons, Paul and Thom, work with us at our ranch with their families. We love them. There's no end of our love for them. However, we have committed to never give them counsel unless they ask for it—not about their children, not about their marriage, not about their finances, not about anything in their lives.

If we see something from our vantage point that is very, very destructive in their lives, we will, at the right time and in the right way, approach them and say, "We love you, and we are praying for you. Because of those things, we wanted you to know that we see this going on, but we won't get involved unless you say okay. Know that we are here for you, if you need anything." We open the door for them to come to us if they want to talk about the issue, but that is all we do. Beyond that, it is up to them. We have never had to do that, fortunately, but we are certainly willing to approach it from that vantage point.

The reason we don't offer counsel, and we don't give them advice about anything unless they ask for it, is that if we did that continually, our kids would resent such intrusions. They might begin to think that we don't believe they are capable of handling things on their own, which isn't true.

So much of the time with grandparents, as with parents, it's never enough. We once counseled a young woman who said, "I can never do enough to please my dad. I can never be good enough. I can never love the Lord enough. In everything that he says to me, there is always a 'but' at the end. 'You are doing great, but—' and so on and so forth." We think it is very important that parents know they can't keep raising the bar for their children. Their kids don't want to hear a "but" every time they give them a compliment or edify them. We should never have a "but" at the end of our compliments. Edify your children, and just leave it at that.

3) *Always remember who your child is marrying becomes as much your child as your own child.*

Your son-in-law becomes your son, and your daughter-in-law becomes your daughter. Why? Because the two have become one flesh. If they are one, how can you see it as my son and my daughter-in-law, or vice versa? You have to see it as your son and your daughter, because they are one in Christ. They have become one flesh, and you must see each of them with the same affection. We try with all of our hearts—and I think we do it pretty well—to love, edify, encourage, incentivize, bless, in every way, our daughters and our sons, no matter which of them are our natural-born children. They all call us Mom and Dad, and we treat them like our very own.

4) *God can handle them better than you can.*

That is why praying for your married children, loving them, encouraging them, appreciating them, and blessing them will go a long way toward turning them over to God and letting God, in His wisdom, get them the help that they need. Remember, they are going to go through some of the same stuff you went through, some of the same challenges that you have gone through, and if you are wiser for what you have experienced, they will be too. We promise you, if you leave them up to God, not jump in prematurely, and let them work it out, they will learn for themselves. We have both said, "One of the best things newlyweds can do is move away from both sets of parents for the first five years and learn how to need each other, love each other, and work through the challenges they have on their own."

Then, finally, I always tell the parents, "One day, as your children grow older and God gives them children, your dreams will come true when they come to you and say, 'I'm sorry, you were right.' That will be a day you will always cherish. Just be available to them. Don't jump in unsolicited, and the joy of being their parent will continue on and on, and you will have talks like you never had before."

We can honestly say that makes it all worthwhile!

Chapter Seventeen

A Very Personal Word from Paul and Billie Kaye

Don't miss the journey. Boys will become men, and girls women. Don't miss the eye-to-eye conversations, the running through the house loudly. The journey gets sweeter. I've loved listening to Don speaking life into my men on this trip home. Yeah, we still get eye to eye; we get real with each other and run loudly through the house like a bunch of crazy folk. I must say this has been a trip worth taking. If I can encourage young families to take time. To stop. Look eye to eye. Dads speak to your sons (real talk), Mom speak to your girls (real talk), and play together. Take the journey!
—Don Jr. and KK Balltzglier, personal friends who
wrote to us after taking a vacation with their family

From Paul

Growing up was not easy for me. I look back and remember what a rebellious son I was. But at the same time, I really don't recall any times of real mentorship or guidance from my parents, especially my dad. I'm not trying to assign blame or play the victim, but parenting for the most part was missing from our home.

My dad worked hard and we always had provision. My mom was great at cooking, cleaning, and taking care of our needs. But parenting is about so much more than that. It's about verbal communication—saying, "I love you," and meaning it. It's about listening to your children and meaning it. It's about talking about their future and truly being interested. It's about providing moral guidance, not you telling your children that they are an embarrassment to you as parents. It's about teaching them who God is and letting them know how He loves them; taking them to church, not just sending them. It's being an example of God's love, kindness, forgiveness, patience, and care.

It's not telling your children they'll never amount to anything and will end up one day in prison. It's not seeing them leave for the Marine Corps and telling them you're glad they're leaving. It's not losing your temper and pounding their head into the floor and having their mother try to pull you off of them.

It's not Dad slapping your mother with a wallet, calling her names, leaving in the car and abandoning you both, only to come back minutes later, shove an ice cream cone in your face, and call you a bastard. It's not watching your child then throw up, driving in silence for five miles, and then dropping your child off at the office of a YMCA camp for six weeks of the summer. It's not telling your child to go in and check to see if his name's on the arrival list when he still smells of fresh vomit on his shirt, and then leaving his luggage on the porch and driving away before he comes back to say goodbye.

It's not when you're about to go off to Reform School in Windham, Maine, and you ask your dad the ultimate question while sitting on the couch waiting to be picked up. "Dad, do you think that God's real?" only for him to reply, "Nah, that's for sissies and weak people."

And it's not about spending the next twenty years trying not to be a sissy or a weakling.

Nope, that's not the way it's supposed to be. For many years I dealt with a myriad of challenges because of my childhood—insecurity, hatred, immorality, bitterness, and feeling generally worthless. I spent most of my life trying to prove I had worth and value. Even after I married Billie Kaye and had children, I was still a major disaster.

BUT GOD...

When God stepped in, my life changed and He started me on the way to wholeness. I am so thankful for God's mercy, grace, kindness, patience, forgiveness, and love. My point is that these are the same qualities that God wants you to demonstrate to your children—teaching them, training them, encouraging them, and preparing them for adulthood and their futures.

I wished I had grown up closer with my siblings, because now I would be closer to their children. But parents make that happen. Not that grown children are not responsible for their own choices, but parents can either promote unity and invest in making that happen or live consumed with themselves and watch it deteriorate. I'm not saying that your children will always be best friends, but there is a loyalty in our family that binds our hearts together. I see it every time we get together.

Billie and I don't always see eye to eye with our children and they don't always see eye to eye with us, but there is a fierce loyalty in our family that runs very deep. We have spent time, energy, resources, and whatever else is necessary to make that happen. Our children are experiencing raising their own children and have learned and grown from our mistakes. They are all better parents and spouses than Billie and me—but that's the way it's supposed to be. You're not in competition with your children. You're their parents, their guide, and their elevator to lift them to greater heights.

Ever since Billie and I married, I wanted more than anything for our family to be very close. I wanted our children to grow up close and for Billie and me to always be a very important part of their lives, even after they married. I didn't know how to make that happen, but coming to Christ was the first step.

I've made a lot of mistakes, even as a Christian, but one thing my family knows for sure is that we are family. I have tried in a lot of different ways to demonstrate that to them, and they all know, above all my mistakes, they are my life, and that I will do anything I can to maintain that closeness.

Love deeply and passionately. Forgive quickly and completely. Give freely and abundantly to your children, and your life will be full and complete as you grow old.

FROM BILLIE

As Paul and I were finishing this book, we asked each other a couple of questions: "Why do our grown, married children enjoy spending time with us? What have we done right to make that happen?" Rather than answer the question ourselves, we decided to ask each one of them.

Their replies blessed my heart so greatly. I can assure you, I have so much gratitude in my heart to the Lord for His mercy and kindness to grant me the privilege and blessing of being their mother. Nothing on this earth warms my heart more than seeing them grow up, raise their families, and serve Him.

So, here are the responses we got from the *six* children God blessed us with:

> *You are fun—an example of what I want with Mark. You give good advice and don't judge. You're just my parents and I love you. I enjoy your company. You don't pressure us or make us feel guilty if we don't do what you want.*
>
> *I did not really know my grandparents and I missed that. Other kids talked about theirs growing up, and I saw grandparents with their grandkids, and I wanted that for my kids. You want to be around us and want a relationship with me. Bottom line: I love you!*
>
> —GRETCHEN ANN TSIKA RUSH

The reasons I enjoy/love spending time with you both are many. You have both taught me many things in regard to being the man God wants me to be. I always come away after being with you feeling exhorted, encouraged, challenged, and sharpened. I also enjoy time with you because I feel like I can be myself. Knowing you accept me for who I am, not who you want me to be. This does not mean that you don't work to chip away some of me, but I believe you know that God is ultimately the one who must change me. You are fun to be with and I always enjoy hanging out with you!

Ultimately I love you because I love my wife greatly. And I know that loving her means loving those who are very import-ant to her. All that, I believe, glorifies Christ and honors you.

—MARK ALAN RUSH

I feel like you truly love my family. We have your full support in what we choose to do in life. Nothing will separate us from you and your love. We feel that daily. Both of you complete each other to make great parents and grandparents.

—THOMAS JAMES TSIKA

It's because you both love me unconditionally. I actually "feel" that when I'm around you. Since the day we met you've made me feel comfortable and safe—isn't that a parent's job? I love you both. :-)

—KELLEY LYNNE TSIKA

Loyalty is the word that comes to mind. Why loyalty? Loyalty has been engrained in me since my youth. There is a loyalty that I feel to and from Mom and Dad that goes far beyond disagree-ments, frustrations, or idiosyncrasies. Due to that loyalty, you encourage and motivate us to be together often.

—PAUL EDWARD TSIKA II

You have not ever treated me like an outsider, but always like a daughter. You love and accept me, even though you know I am not perfect. You honor me in front of my children and others.

—MELANIE ELAINE TSIKA

Paul and I want to invest in our children and grandchildren—and now our great-grandchildren! We don't want to keep everything, but we want to share it with them while we're alive. We have faith also that time in Heaven will be everything and more that God promises. But we have a great desire to spend time with them here and now. We want to be a part of their lives while we can, and we work hard at communicating that to them.

FROM BOTH OF US

One day Billie and Gretchen were talking, and Billie was sharing with her that, "When you really love your children, they don't remember the bad." Then Billie added, "Like the times I was angry and raised my voice to you."

Gretchen said, "Mom, I don't ever remember you doing that!"

Billie replied, "I rest my case."

Dear friends, we pray you will take away from this book that there is hope for you. We pray you've been informed, encouraged, and inspired. Children are very resilient and will not remember much of what we remember as their parents. But all the same, never forget to be quick to frequently say, "I'm sorry, please forgive me. I love you."

In some ways, we think parents and children raise each other. We fixed things the children broke when they were young, and now that we're older, they're fixing whatever we've broken. All the same, ultimately we know that our God is in charge and can always be trusted. So be encouraged as you *Parent with Purpose.*

ABOUT PAUL AND BILLIE KAYE TSIKA

For ministry information plus additional
DVDs and CD sets—

Paul E. Tsika Ministries Inc.
P.O. Box 136
Midfield, Texas 77458
Office: 361:588-7190
Web site: www.plowon.org

OTHER BOOKS BY PAUL AND BILLIE KAYE TSIKA

PAUL TSIKA

Sequoia-Size Success (unlocking your potential for greatness)

What You Seed Is What You Get (seeding your way to success)

39 Days of Destiny (devotions for destiny achievers)

Releasing Your Full Potential (our potentials are God-given)

Flying Right Side Up in an Upside Down World
(negotiating life's turbulence)

Understanding Your New Life (first steps for new Believers)

Handfuls of Purpose (the story of Ruth)

BILLIE KAYE TSIKA

Operation Blessing (speaking blessings into the lives of our families)

Dining with the Diamonds (a collection of interesting recipes with funny
stories from great friends)

GET THESE OTHER GREAT RESOURCES

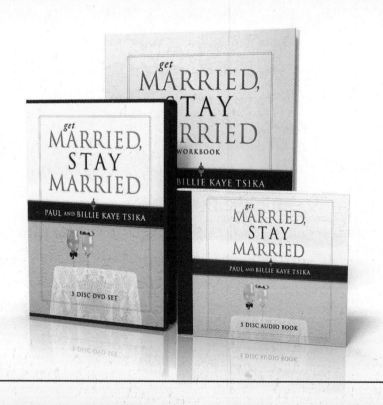